Rescue Mission

Rescue Mission: Prisoners of Darkness

ANGELA Y. ATTIAH

KINGDOM ALLY

United in Power & Purpose

While the author has made every effort to provide accurate Internet addresses at the time of publication, neither the publisher nor the author assumes any responsibility for errors or changes that occur after publication. Further, the publisher does not have any control over and does not assume any responsibility for author or third-party Web sites or their content.

ISBN: 1-9769605-5-X

Printed in the United States of America

DEDICATION

I dedicate this book to you, the reader, for taking a brave step towards the beautiful and life-changing gift of healing and reconciliation. May your journey to wholeness serve as a testimony of God's grace, mercy, and unconditional love!

Acknowledgements

My deepest gratitude goes to our loving and gracious Lord Jesus Christ, for commissioning me to write this book, in order to bring knowledge to set other captives free.

I am also eternally grateful for all the teachers, mentors, and friends who have shaped and guided my life along the way.

It is also with heartfelt appreciation for my three amazing children, Luke, Brody, and Zarrah, who inspire me with their remarkable resilience through the personal sacrifices that were endured in birthing this labor of love.

Last, but certainly not least, I am overwhelmed with gratitude for my father, Jack. He has become a trustworthy vessel of God's great humility and wisdom, as he stewards and shares the valuable spiritual lessons he learns. His love and devotion to God has not been without tremendous sacrifice, but as the Good Book conveys, "those who have been forgiven much, love much." (Luke 7:47)

Personal Letter to God

Dear Lord Jesus,

Thank you for my life and the experiences I have conquered because of your faithfulness in pursuing me, even in the times I chose to reject you or was ignorant of your ways.

How can I ever fully comprehend the depths of your love and the lengths to which you have gone to save me, when I clearly deserved punishment?

I whole-heartedly thank you that I have lived through sexual assault, a suicide attempt, domestic violence, self-hatred, addiction, injustice by the family court system, homelessness, rejection by family and friends, and countless other dangerous snares.

Not by my own strength, but by your Holy Spirit I am healed and shielded from the pain of each and every one of these occurrences. I am thankful because it is by these experiences that a bridge is formed between myself and others being held in captivity by similar physical, emotional, mental and spiritual torment.

Send me as your messenger, O God, to rescue the voiceless, discarded, and even the violent souls who are crying out for redemption and freedom from the sin and oppression in their lives!

For it is not your will that anyone should perish, but that all would come to realize and accept the free gift of abundant grace, peace, and joy you offer.

Lord Jesus, I am so grateful you are not a man that will ever disappoint me. Your sacrificial and unconditional love truly does cast out all fear, deliver us from evil, and heal our brokenness. It is only in you that we are granted victory over the evil forces of this world.

All the remaining days of my life, I will joyfully and boldly celebrate the peace and rest that comes by knowing you personally, which is a priceless treasure bestowed on all who seek you with their whole heart. I adore and need you always.

Your beloved,

Angela

TABLE OF CONTENTS

Introduction

Is it possible for someone who commits sexual violence against a child to be completely redeemed and transformed into the likeness of Jesus Christ? And can that child ever truly recover from such a heinous act? This first hand account of healing and reconciliation, between father and daughter, offers the inspiration and guidance to believe that *all things are possible through God.*

With the ever-growing reports of sexual and domestic violence running rampant in our society, it's high time we address the root cause of this worldwide epidemic. Unless we eradicate the wounds lodged deep within our souls, brought on by past traumatic experiences and generational sin, we remain vulnerable to physical, emotional, and mental torment. The reality is, there's an invisible realm of dark spirits that desire to express themselves through human hosts, and they use soul wounds and sin to gain access.

Contrary to popular belief, even self-proclaimed Christians can suffer from these evil invasions, especially if they embrace the lie that believers are powerless against sin. It is only in partnership with the Holy Spirit, through our faith in Jesus Christ, that we are able to pursue a holy life and have victory over the darkness in this world. This book offers a framework for healing and purifying the soul, in order to take hold of one's destiny and restore what has been stolen by these dark forces.

May this book enlighten your spiritual senses to witness the supernatural and transforming power available to all who pursue a personal relationship with Jesus Christ, while pushing past the religious walls erected by manmade agendas. The Lord is faithful to reveal Himself to those who diligently seek Him.

The magnitude of possibilities for a new, abundant, and adventurous life awaits you!

Helpful Tools

At the end of each chapter, you'll find a section to jot down any notes, questions, or memories that may surface as you are reading.

I encourage you to use these as conversation points with God, especially if you are training to identify his voice. Journaling has been such a powerful tool for me personally in learning to talk with God.

Remember, nothing is hidden from God so choose to be vulnerable with Him. He already knows everything in your heart and His greatest desire is to build a trusting relationship with you—yes, YOU!

***

"If you look for me wholeheartedly, you will find me. I will be found by you," says the Lord.

Jeremiah 29:13-14 NLT

Chapter 1: Exciting Explorations

As a nine year old kid growing up in the small town of Dallas, Georgia, there was freedom and safety in exploring all avenues of our moderately sized neighborhood. Even the dense forest at the end of the street was fertile ground for hours of imaginary adventures.

Each day after homework and chores were done, a posse of kids would gather in the cul-de-sac in front of our house to vote on how we would make the most of the remaining daylight. We played hard until hearing the sound of mom's whistle beckoning us back inside for supper.

My parents were fun loving people who filled our free time with softball games, boat rides on the lake, go cart racing and monster truck rallies. My (adopted) dad, Rick, was actively involved in coaching me in softball and we spent countless hours together playing catch in the front yard.

With each toss of the ball he would share nuggets of wisdom about life and how to conduct myself in honoring ways. As a former marine, he was strict with discipline and chores, which taught me valuable work ethic and accountability skills, yet he also had a very playful and lighthearted side to his personality.

My mom, Christie, is one of the sweetest gals you'll ever meet. Her smile radiates with such warmth and fun-loving conversations. Don't attempt to wrong her family in any way though or else you'll suffer the wrath of a ferocious mama bear!

She and my biological father, Jack, were married very young, at only sixteen and twenty-one, respectively. My mom married to escape an abusive home life, and my father wanted children to carry on his family line. I was a planned pregnancy and arrived just a year after they were married.

Before my first birthday, however, their marriage quickly disintegrated under extremely hostile and abusive circumstances, proving impossible to stabilize on the sinking foundation of sand that stood beneath them.

They both were harboring horrific pain from traumatic childhood experiences that had never been dealt with, which only intensified the fire of their explosive arguments.

My mom fled with me out of state, filed for divorce, and within a few months after the separation, she met Rick.

She was upfront about her circumstances and he honored her by waiting until the divorce was final before asking her out. Just before my third birthday, they were married and my adorable, chubby cheeked baby brother, Rickey, arrived 6 months later.

From that point on, Rick became dad to me and eventually adopted me when I turned 12.

Having experienced the separation from my biological father at such a young age, and with limited ongoing involvement, any memories I had with him quickly faded. The next time I would see him was when I was nine years old, and it would prove to be a traumatic, life-altering encounter.

Curiosity

It was the spring of 1981 and my baby sister, Nicole, was nearly a year old. She was absolutely the highlight of my young life! Coli, as we affectionately called her, was *my* baby and I spent hours cuddling and talking with her after school.

She had the most contagious laugh! She would lay on the floor and roar with belly bouncing giggles as I tossed a babydoll up in the air. For show-and-tell at school that year, I proudly demonstrated my doll tossing skills and shared stories of our little adventures together.

One Sunday morning, as I was feeding Coli her bottle, I looked out the window and noticed a white school bus picking up families in the neighborhood. I asked mom about the bus and she explained the neighbors were all going to church. "What's church?" I asked curiously.

I don't recall her exact response, but I clearly understood that church was not a place our family would be going, other than for the occasional wedding or funeral.

It is my personal belief that my parents have been deeply hurt by people who claimed to be Christians, making it inconceivable to them that God could be real—and if He was real, then they believed He was not a loving God for allowing painful events to transpire in their lives.

Now my parents are honest, good natured people. They raised me to care about folks and to treat others the way I want to be treated. Anyone who knows them, boasts of their kind hearts and strong integrity. Plus I've never witnessed two people love and respect each other so deeply as my mom and dad do.

Well, I was a curious kid who asked a plethora of questions—to my mother's dismay at times—and I wanted to know more about what all these families were doing each week. My mom simply didn't have the answers to give me about church, and ultimately, about God, so I began asking around in the neighborhood.

In spite of my parents' personal beliefs about a non-existent or uncaring God, they did honor my desire to explore church when I asked to go with my best friend, Terry, one Sunday. That day turned out to be an amazing gift and major turning point in my young life!

Terry and I always had fun, riding motor bikes, swimming, going line dancing and acting out heroic movie scenes. So when she invited me to church, I was ecstatic! I really had no idea what to expect, and was filled with curiosity in finally seeing what all the commotion was about.

The Big Reveal

Sunday finally arrived and I was bursting with excitement to go to church. I imagined myself stepping into the building and being magically transported into some wild new adventure. *"What was God like?"* I pondered.

Something about engaging with the Creator of the entire universe had my insides bouncing with joyful anticipation!

I recall entering into a white walled room filled with dark wood accents and us taking a seat near the back right section. It was a simple gathering place, but something about it just felt special. To this day, I contribute my deep affection for old wood furniture to the experience in that place.

My attention was drawn to a picture of a man hanging by his hands and feet on a cross, with thorns around his head. *Who would do such a thing and why was it being displayed in a church?* These were the types of questions rattling around in my head.

While everyone was shaking hands and greeting one another, the place suddenly grew quiet as an ordinary looking man approached the podium. He had a confidence about him, but not in an arrogant sort of way.

From the moment he began speaking, I found myself on the very edge of my seat, intently captivated by the mere sound of his voice. He told the story about a man named Jesus and how he came to save the world by dying a horrific death on the cross. *So that's why the picture was there!*

I felt like I could sit in that pew for hours, listening as the descriptive accounts of Jesus' life, death, and resurrection played out in my imagination. Then the man said by just believing these stories were real, Jesus would come make himself known to me personally and make me a better person?

Why would anyone say no to that?

When the preacher asked if anyone was ready to invite Jesus into their own hearts, everything inside of me wanted to run to him and wave my hand, as if to say, *"I do! I do!"* But I hesitated to see what everyone else was doing. After all, I was a first timer at church and a mere kid.

Once I saw a few people stand up and walk towards the preacher, I quickly glanced over to Terry's mom who gave me the go ahead nod. Like a kid dashing towards the gates of Disneyland, I rushed down the aisle to where I was quickly joined by a crowd of other folks.

The preacher led us all through a prayer with words that truly seemed to drench my body in pure joy. It felt like I had just won the lottery of love! It was a simple prayer—not one of any remarkable eloquence, but with words that resonated so deep within me. It went something like this:

God, I'm a sinner and need you to save me. I believe you sent Jesus to pay the price for my wrongdoings with his death on the cross, and that you raised him back to life three days later. I profess Jesus Christ is Lord and receive the power of the Holy Spirit to fill me so I can live a life worthy of my calling. In Jesus name I pray. Amen.

Afterwards, all the adults around me were crying and praising God, whereas I felt a giddiness and excitement of getting to know Jesus more! Years later, however, I would discover those were tears of inexpressible gratitude they had cried for the complete forgiveness of all the wrongs they had committed.

I learned for myself, later in life, that a huge invisible weight is lifted in that moment, when you finally release the burdens of guilt and shame. God is so gracious to take it all away from you when you come to him.

Power Jolt

After service we went back to Terry's house, where she and I were in her room talking about the whole experience. I was still so giddy and could hardly contain my excitement, hours after the service had ended.

As I was retelling my story to Terry, I pointed up to heaven in gratitude towards God and suddenly felt an electric jolt of some sort go straight through my entire body.

"What was that?" I asked fearfully.

Quite frankly, it felt dangerously similar to the time I tried to deposit a penny into the electrical outlet, which resulted in a strong shock and a firm reprimand from my mom. Immediately, I felt like I had done something wrong. Terry had no idea what I was talking about because she hadn't felt or seen anything.

After talking with Terry's mom, the initial excitement and joy quickly returned once I learned it was actually a touch from God's Holy Spirit.

Wow! Can you even imagine? God touched ME? I felt so special and loved. It still blows my mind to know we have such a personal God.

When I got back home, I told my parents all about what had happened. And while they seemed genuinely happy it was an enjoyable experience for me, they must have thought it was all part of my imagination, because all I got in response was, "Hmmm, glad you had fun sweetheart." It was the same case with many of my friends at school—no one seemed to understand what I was talking about.

I've learned it's down right impossible for someone to comprehend the immense feeling of love and power that surges through your body, unless you've experienced a touch from God for yourself.

Trust me, it's not just for the religious "elite" either —remember, I was only nine years old at the time. There's a reason God calls us to have childlike faith in him.

I don't recall going back to church with the Terry's family after that encounter, as summer approached and our Sundays were filled with other family commitments. However, I often thought about what had happened to me that day, as my foundational belief in God was formed.

Heightened Awareness

That electric jolt I felt at Terry's house that day must have rewired something in my brain, because afterwards, I began to have very vivid dreams. I always felt there was some sort of hidden message in them, but couldn't quite grasp what I was suppose to do about them.

Many of my dreams involved having the ability to fly or utilizing supernatural powers to defeat or escape monsters. Little did I know that God was training me for what was already taking place in the unseen realm.

Many times I experienced deja vu and then remembered dreaming about that same exact situation. Did you know that one-third of the Bible is actually made up of God speaking through dreams and visions? And considering a third of our lives are spent asleep, perhaps we should be paying more attention to the dreams we are having.

I'm not suggesting all dreams are from God— some are in response to our current emotional state, or based on the chemical nature of what we ate before bed. But then there are those dreams that are just so memorable!

The one thing to know is that our dreams often give guidance or require a response, and the only way to interpret their meaning is in prayerful partnership with Holy Spirit. Any other method of interpretation will completely skew the true meaning.

Calling Seed Planted

Another interesting phenomenon began to happen. I was suddenly able to see past the tough exterior of the bullies at my school, and would ponder what might actually motivate them to lash out against others.

Even at a young age, I deduced that it had to be because of something that was causing them sorrow. It became my mission to show them love and kindness in order to soften their hardened hearts— something I've carried with me even to this day!

I also found myself drawn to the outcasts in school —those who sat alone at lunch, were picked on, or who seemed to carry some sort of sadness within them. It was so rewarding to watch their dark moods transform into brightness with a genuine smile and confidence building conversation pointing out their worth. Most of the time, they were sad because they simply felt invisible to the world around them.

How many of us feel that way today, even with the plethora of social media platforms?

I believe it is wired deep within our human nature to belong to a community—one that interacts face-to-face. Isolation is a harsh form of punishment, which is why prisons often use it for the unruly. That is not a place I ever considered being, but later in life, that is exactly where the Lord would call me to go. Are you surprised to learn that Jesus wants to pour out his love and forgiveness on prisoners?

Little did I realize that even at the age of nine, the Lord was preparing my heart for a calling in the ministry of reconciliation. Extending forgiveness to others who have hurt you is the first step, and often the most difficult one to take. There is such a powerful explosion of love, peace, and joy that flows from reconciliation! Many times, it is overcoming the disappointments we face that serve as the bridge to connecting with and helping others. Let's just say, I've had a lot of painful bridges constructed from my own experiences. We all have. No one is exempt from pain and trials in this life. It's how we deal with the disappointments that ultimately shapes our character.

Personal Reflections

***

For everyone who calls on the name of the Lord will be saved.

Romans 10:13 NLT

Chapter 2: Traumatic Traps

Summer was my favorite part of the year, as is typical for most kids, and also a time when I was most actively involved with softball. So when my mom informed me that I was going to be staying with my father Jack for half of the summer, I was absolutely devastated and felt like she was punishing me for something.

I thought, *"Why do I have to leave my family to go stay with someone I don't even know?"* It felt completely unfair, and at the time, I simply didn't understand she was merely following court orders.

Looking back, I can see how the timing of accepting Jesus played a significant role in enduring what was to come during my time away from home.

When the day finally arrive, I nervously climbed into my father's Volkswagen Van. I don't remember much about the ride from Georgia to Kentucky, except that it was agonizingly long and filled me with anxiety. All I kept thinking was, *"I just want to go home."*

Once we arrived at his place, I spent most of the month with his mom and my younger half brother and sister. We had fun together, and I was treated kindly, but I was utterly homesick for my family and friends back in Georgia.

Bedtime was especially tough for me and when I felt the most alone. Many nights I would cry myself to sleep or be woken up suddenly with strange new thoughts that terrorized me.

"Nobody loves you."

"Your mom shipped you off to get rid of you."

"Your father doesn't even want to be with you."

"Your family is having more fun without you."

"I bet they wouldn't even miss you if you were dead!"

What was going on? Where were these invading thoughts coming from? I just wanted to get back to the familiar surroundings of my home in Georgia, back to some sort of normalcy. However, each day seemed to drag on longer than the previous, until finally the last day arrived. That's when my innocence was stolen and everything in my world came crashing down in a paralyzing halt.

Fear Paralysis

I remember sitting on the couch in the dimly lit family room of my father's house. Immediately, an intense fear came over me and my heart began to pound with anticipation because I had hardly spent any time with him over the past month, much less alone.

When I did see him, he was so insistent that I call him "daddy," which seemed disloyal to Rick, so it caused deep tension in my heart. The best I could do was offer a half spoken "diddy" when addressing him.

As we sat across from one another on the couch, I could smell a strong odor of alcohol. Before I could make out what he was saying, he began to rub my leg, moving closer and closer to my inner thigh. I was scared and confused about what was happening. No one had ever touched me like that. It literally felt like my heart was going to jump right out of my chest!

Then all of a sudden he was on top of me. Sheer panic set in and I completely froze. Everything inside of me wanted to push him off and run away, but physically I couldn't move—partly because he was weighing me down, but mostly because of the paralyzing fear that covered the air like a thick canopy. I was crying and screaming on the inside, but no sound was coming out of my mouth, as if I had an invisible gag.

As he pressed himself against my pubic bone, all I kept thinking was, *"Oh no! I'm going to die and I'll never see my family again! Mom...dad....I need you! Help me...please...heeeelp!"*

Reality set in and I knew they couldn't help me being hundreds of miles away. Desperation took over as I realized I would never feel my mom's hugs or the touch of her tender kisses on my cheek again. Nor would I hear my baby sister's laugh again, see my baby brother, or play catch with my dad. It felt like my life was over.

Saving Grace

In the midst of my short nine years of life flashing before my eyes, out of nowhere, the story of Jesus I had heard at Terry's church came flooding back. I even thought I heard a faint whisper say, "Call out to me and I will save you." *Was that Jesus talking to me?* It was hard to tell because the whisper was more like an impression in my heart than hearing an audible voice. Plus, the pounding of my heart was almost deafening.

A surge of courage welled up within me and, with silent tears streaming down my face, I forced out the faintest whisper, "Stop…please…stop. I want to go home. Please help me Jesus." At that very moment, my father sat up abruptly, stared at me with a bizarre look in his eyes, then hurried off to his room without saying another word to me.

Was it over? I sat there shaking so intensely on the couch for what seemed like hours, afraid to even breathe. *What just happened? Did I imagine that? Did Jesus really save me?*

The next morning I was jolted awake by the sound of my father's voice calling me into his room. Nervously, I came and stood at his door.

He began talking about the large jar of change sitting next to his bed. Naively, I thought it was for me, but when he said it wasn't, I was filled with deep disappointment. Noticing my expression, he reached into his wallet and handed me a $20 bill.

As I reached for it, he held onto the money. While staring intently into my eyes, he sternly told me not to tell anyone what had happened the night before. As I shyly whispered "ok," he released the bill into my hand. After a quick walk across the street to say goodbye to my grandparents, he placed my suitcase in the back of his van, and drove me back to Georgia.

Utterly relieved to be back home, I ran and jumped into my mom's arms after he dropped me off in the cul-de-sac of my neighborhood. I was sobbing with gratitude to see her again—mom kept asking me if I was alright. I thought for a second about telling her what had happened, but I wasn't even sure where to begin.

Remembering the sternness of my father's warning, I quickly pushed the incident far back into the recesses of my mind. *What would he do if I told them?* I was afraid something bad would happen so I chose to just forget about it.

More than thirty years passed before I would come face-to-face with him again, in an epic explosion of emotions.

Salted Wounds

For several weeks after being back home, my dad Rick asked me why I was calling him "diddy." I had inadvertently modified "daddy" because of the awkwardness I felt with addressing Jack. Maybe it was my imagination, but it seemed like my dad was treating me differently than before the trip. He seemed distant and annoyed with me.

Did he somehow know what had happened? Did he wish I was still gone? These were the thoughts that repeatedly swarmed my mind.

One day after school, dad was home unusually early from his construction job. He agreed to let me go swimming at Terry's house, which was always such a treat, especially during the hot Georgia summers. Terry had a huge swimming pool, motorcycles, and all sorts of cool games to play with in her fit-for-a-princess bedroom.

After a few hours of swimming, my dad called and said it was time for me to come home. Terry and I walked back, talking and laughing the whole way, which usually only took about ten to fifteen minutes. Sometimes longer, if a rabbit or stray cat happen to draw our attention.

When I arrived back home, dad seemed very agitated with me. I realized I didn't have my bathing suit in hand, so he sent me back to Terry's to get it with a stern warning to come right back.

Arriving back at Terry's, I couldn't find my bathing suit right away, and after searching all over the bedroom, I discovered her mom had thrown it in the wash. She threw it in a plastic bag and sent me out the door.

I can't say that I was in a major hurry to get back home, but for a kid, time is really not a pressing matter. As soon as I walked back into the house, dad met me at the door and grabbed my arm, pulling me close to an angry glare, demanding to know what took me so long. I tried explaining that Terry's mom had put it in the wash, but it seemed he really didn't want to hear it.

With one hand still firmly wrapped around my bicep, he unbuckled his belt, slid it through the loops of his jeans and reared back like a rodeo cowboy on a raging bull. Each whip of the belt burned against my bare skin, and was separated only by the pauses between his clenched teeth, "I…told…you…to… come…right…back!   Didn't…I…tell…you…to… come…right…back?   Next…time…you'll…listen… to…me!"

I had experienced my fair share of spankings before, but not even close to the same intensity and force as this one.

Breathless and seemingly satisfied, he sent me to my bedroom. As I lay on my bed stunned by what had just happened, trying to make sense of what I did to deserve such a severe punishment, the same dark thoughts, from the long nights at my father Jack's house, returned.

"You're so stupid. Can't you follow simple directions? Nobody wants you here. You're better off dead!"

I felt utterly dejected as I gingerly felt the angry marks, which wrapped around my skinny legs and covered both my arms from where I tried to block the blows. I lay there with those horrible thoughts turning over and over in my mind until I fell asleep.

Some time later, I awoke to my mom wanting to talk. As soon as I saw her, I wrapped my arms around her neck and began sobbing. She must have thought I was being dramatic because she kept saying, "Oh calm down, it's alright." But as she pulled my arms from around her neck, I winced with pain, and that's when she noticed the marks covering my body.

Like a lioness protecting her cub, she stormed out of the room towards my dad, demanding an explanation. Dad obviously hadn't realized just how hard he had struck me until he came in to see for himself. There was nothing he could say to calm her down.

Amidst the screaming, mom quickly threw some clothes in a bag and rushed us out to the car. We stayed at a family friend's place that night. At times, I could overhear their conversations at the kitchen table.

Mom was adamant that she would not let me go through the same abuse she endured from her stepmom as a child. Plus she had already left one abusive husband and would not stand to be with another.

One moment she was tough minded, and in the next should would cry to her friend saying, "What am I going to do?" It is a familiar struggle for many that tends to cycle through the generations.

After a day or so, we came back home. I could see the intense remorse on my dad's face and actually felt bad for how he was feeling. It's interesting how those same guilty feelings would be met with timely whispers later in life, disguised as false humility, in order to keep me trapped in an abusive marriage.

"Oh just forgive him already and make peace."

"It's over now. There's no since in harping on the past."

"If you would just try harder, he wouldn't have anything to complain about."

While my dad offered a very sincere and heartfelt apology, vowing never to hurt me like that again—which he absolutely never did—something inside of me had changed. A deep sense of fear and disappointment had rooted far down into the cavity of my heart.

Perhaps in and of itself, an event like that may not have had the same affect on me, especially with his sincere apology, but it had occurred so soon after the sexual assault by my father.

Prison of Perfection

From that moment on, it seemed I was afraid of making any mistakes and sought constant approval from my parents, teachers, and friends. Striving to be what I thought other people wanted or needed me to be, in order to gain their approval.

It was mentally exhausting and often left me feeling disappointed and unfulfilled. Nothing ever seemed to satisfy that longing in my heart to feel accepted and loved unconditionally.

As punishment for doing wrong, my parents would often ignore me or express how disappointed they were in me. Again, not that these responses themselves are wrong, but since I was operating from a shattered view of my self-worth, they were like daggers that cut deep within my heart.

In an effort to avoid rejection, at all costs, I formed an unhealthy habit of placing unreasonable demands on myself to be perfect, especially with schoolwork, often feeling like a failure with anything less than an A. I had a reputation of being teacher's pet and getting good grades, so everyone assumed I was this squeaky clean kid who did nothing wrong—yet inside I felt so dirty and worthless.

Living as the only child in our family that didn't share the same dad, I often felt like the black sheep. When my parents talked with me about my dad Rick adopting me, I was all for it—finally I would be an official part of the family!

I was so happy when that day arrived! When my parents asked what I wanted to do to celebrate, I chose going back to school because I was so excited to share the news with all my friends. The whole experience made me feel special and chosen.

Interestingly though, those dark thoughts have a way of degrading anything good in your life, if you give too much attention to them. More and more frequently, I felt torn between two worlds—happy in one moment, celebrating my adoption, then out of nowhere being covered with these dark thoughts about myself again.

"Your dad [Rick] just feels sorry for you."

"Your father [Jack] doesn't want anything to do with you."

"No matter how hard you try, you'll never fit in."

"You are a worthless disappointment to everyone."

As I grew older, my focus turned towards being overly concerned with how I looked, constantly comparing myself to others and, not only wanting to change the things I didn't like about myself, but actually despising any unique traits that I carried.

I just wanted to blend in with everyone else. It was my way of hiding the beauty of who God created me to be. I escaped into the fantasy world of books and movies, daydreaming about how I would be different when I was older. Like most kids who are dissatisfied, I was in such a hurry to grow up.

Looking back on these experiences, I can clearly see I was putting so much effort into earning love, making it a conditional transaction. Later in life, when I reconnected with Jesus, it took considerable time for me to finally accept his unconditional love for me—a love that was not based on what I did *for* God, as an effort to please him, but what I did *with* him that moved his heart.

There are times, even now, I still hear the condemning thoughts that say I'm a failure and a disappointment. That's when I imagine climbing up onto Daddy God's lap so he can hold me close and gently remind me that his love for me is unconditional, even when I make mistakes.

It's no wonder that children often believe their parents don't love them when they are being disciplined. Children of God are no different. As a loving Father, he disciplines us to correct our poor choices and guide us away from danger.

Law of Attraction

Since that fateful night with my father Jack, it was like an invisible sign hung around my neck with, "Easy Target" written on it, which seemed to attract unwanted sexual advances and exploits from creepy neighbors and family friends.

No matter how hard I tried, I felt weak against the deep sense of shame that overwhelmed me each time I allowed someone to touch me inappropriately.

Inside I knew it was wrong, but the need to be liked (or not be rejected) overruled every time. This is what the Bible refers to as the Spirit and the flesh being at war with one another. Until Holy Spirit is the one who leads your steps, the flesh will often gravitate towards sin.

Strangely, even though the sexual advances were unwanted, I started feeling torn between feeling ashamed and enjoying the arousal—a pattern that would lay the foundation for submitting to abusive partners later in life.

Although the sexual advances were unwanted, I would be bombarded with thoughts that weakened my defenses against them.

"How can it be wrong if it feels so good?"

"Your body is the best thing you have to offer."

"Everyone else is doing it. Don't you want to fit in?"

"You're lucky anyone is even paying attention to you."

The statistics on sexual assault are staggering. According to RAINN, the nation's largest sexual violence organization, of sexual abuse cases reported to law enforcement, 93% of juvenile victims knew the perpetrator.

* 59% were acquaintances
* 34% were family members
* 7% were strangers to the victim

By the time I turned 12, I had already encountered multiple sexually related incidents. Masturbation had become a regular outlet of release for all the guilt and shame I felt.

At times, I would hear the gentle inner whisper of God saying, "You don't have to do this my child. Just say no." But by then, the power of the negative thoughts had already taken root in my soul, and I chalked up the memories of my experience with Jesus as a figment of my imagination.

Without being connected into a community of believers, it's like taking a hot coal from the fire. Eventually, the coal completely loses heat the longer it is disconnected from the fire.

Until I later rediscovered that powerful love jolt from God, I sought everything to fill the void inside— sex, drugs, alcohol, money, and all things rebellious. Ultimately, I realized that void could only be filled by the faithful love of our Creator.

Personal Reflections

Personal Reflections

***

For we are not fighting against flesh-and-blood enemies, but against evil rulers and authorities of the unseen world, against mighty powers in this dark world, and against evil spirits in the heavenly places.

Ephesians 6:12 NLT

Chapter 3: Rebellious Roads

As I entered my early teen years, I was often tasked with babysitting my younger siblings, in lieu of being able to partake in the social activities of acceptance a teen longs for.

I remember trying out and making the cheerleading squad—hoping that would catapult my likability factor at school—only to have my parents reject the idea altogether. I was furious and stewed about how unfair it was.

With that incident, something inside of me snapped, *"Doesn't anybody care about what I want?"*

All that un-dealt with pain and rejection bottled up inside served as fertile ground for the raging tsunami of destructive choices that followed over the next few years. Oh how I tormented my parents with lies and deceit, for no other reason than to see if I could get away with it!

Even through it all, Jesus was still calling out for me to come back to him. What a forgiving God who loves us even through the most disgusting parts of our lives. I sure didn't recognize it then, but I look back now with such overwhelming gratitude that he never left me, in spite of my rebellion.

Betrayal

I met my first official boyfriend at a Christian concert held in a local church one Saturday night. My best friend had invited me to go along with her family. As freshman in high school, we were surveying the crowd to see who was there. My friend quickly pointed out a very popular sophomore boy, urging me to go talk with him on her behalf.

After snickering together for some time and planning the approach, I got up the courage to go talk to him for her. Once I got over there, however, and awkwardly gestured back to my friend to express her interest in him, he turned to me and surprisingly said, "Well I am way more interested in you pretty girl!"

I tried to redirect back and tell him how wonderful my friend was, but like a gullible fish, I ultimately took the bait of his smooth talking flattery—hook, line, and sinker!

How could I totally betray my best friend like that?!

All I knew is that it felt good to have the kind of attention he was giving me, especially from someone so popular.

I'd mostly agreed to go talk with him, believing there would be *no reason for him to like me.*

Like an underhanded snake, I slinked back to my friend and lied about the whole conversation, leading her on to believe that he was interested in her.

As the concert started, my focus was taken aback by how many people were singing their hearts out for Jesus. I found it strangely familiar, like trying to recall the face of an old friend, but not quite formulating the details in my mind. I was completely distracted by the earlier conversation. And with the direction my life had taken, I had somehow lost that overwhelming love I felt for Jesus just five years before.

Well as is common for most high schools, dating rumors move like a mighty dust storm, and before school on Monday, the cat was out of the bag that the guy my friend was into actually liked me. Of course, the whole thing caused a wedge between my best friend and I because I chose to go out with him instead of considering her feelings. What nasty things we do to others when we feel so insecure!

Throughout the next year of dating him, seeds of rebellion began to sprout. He was from the other side of the tracks, if you will, and his parents gave him total free reign, which was the complete opposite of mine.

Remember I shared before that my dad had a military background? Well, it felt like I was held under lock and key with chores and babysitting responsibilities. As a protective father, I'm pretty certain he would have chained me in my room if it were legal. At least that's what my "oh woes me, I'm so deprived" thinking told me.

Being responsible parents, mine asked to meet my boyfriend's mom and dad. That gathering did not go over too well. But the clincher came when my boyfriend put his hand on my thigh as we were sitting with my parents.

I could see the masked rage rise up in my dad, like an overwhelming swarm of angry hornets, when he very pointedly suggested my boyfriend remove his hand from my thigh, or else suffer the loss of it.

I was forbidden to see my boyfriend after that, which of course, only made him more appealing to me. I began sneaking out of the house, staying out all night, and skipping school just to be with him. Our young romance was built on the foundation of betrayal, rebellion, and soon after—sex.

Not surprisingly, when going to the bathroom early one morning, a portion of the condom that was used in our rebellious escapades just hours before, had come out of me. I panicked with thoughts of being pregnant. *My parents would absolutely kill me!*

Like she was able to read my mind, my mother said to me that day, "If you're sneaking around with that boy and end up pregnant, don't think you're going to keep the baby."

My mom had been down that hard road of teenage pregnancy. And although she and my father chose to conceive me, she had lived through the burdens of caring for a child as a teenager and as a single mom.

Unbearable Rejection

It was a few months shy of my 15th birthday when my life nearly came to an end after experiencing the ever-traumatic first love break-up. I cornered my boyfriend in the hallway that morning and told him about the condom. He was totally panic stricken by the thought that I might be pregnant.

Although he didn't say it, the expression on his face spoke volumes, *"You're on your own! I'm outta here!"* He avoided me the rest of the day. The haunting thoughts met me full force after that conversation.

"You're such a reject."

"Why would anyone want to stay with you?"

"What a laughing stock you're gonna be with a baby!"

Distraught and rejected, I stayed home from school the next day. Doing all I could to distract myself from the tormenting thoughts, I turned on the TV to find the Oprah Winfrey show.

As soon as they announced the topic was on "Molestation," the mental dam I had built to protect myself suddenly broke loose and the painful memories, from that last night with my father, came flooding back. It had been almost six years since it happened, but it felt like another lifetime ago.

Like a weighty glass vase slamming against the floor, I cried out with piercing anguish as I felt my heart shatter into a million pieces inside my pounding chest. The emotional torment was more than I could physically bear, turning into a heaviness that laid atop my weakened body like a 100 pound sand bag. I thought, *"What was the point of this life when there's so much pain?"*

Battling fiercely with the barrage of suicidal thoughts that swarmed around me like blood thirsty bats, I reached for the gun my dad kept in his nightstand. It was as if my thoughts were on autopilot. The game "Russian Roulette" came to mind.

After a quick spin of the cylinder, I shakily placed the barrel of the gun against my temple and contemplated pulling the trigger. The myriad of dark thoughts continued to bombard me.

"You're a disgusting, worthless loser!"

"Just kill yourself already! You won't be missed at all!"

"What are you waiting for? Just do it! Do it NOW!"

"Come on and do it! Just end all this pain!"

"No one is ever gonna love you after everything you've done!"

Then out of nowhere, I felt something in my heart say, "I love you!" This time, my focus again went abruptly back to that picture of Jesus in the church. *"Could he really love me? How was that even possible after all I had done?"*

Blinded by all the confusion and disappointment, I just couldn't find it in my heart to believe Jesus' words. I thought, *"It's too late. There's too much pain."* And in that moment, I resolved to end it all.

With tears gushing down my face, I was prepared to embrace death, right there in my parents' bedroom —completely alone and feeling devoid of all hope for the future.

The next few seconds moved in slow motion as I curled my finger around the cold trigger, feeling the tautness of the spring. My focus narrowed in on one thought—finally being free from the pain.

I took in a deep breath, believing it would be my last, then let all the air slowly expel from my lungs. *"This is it. They would sure be sorry for hurting me,"* I thought to myself before slowly squeezing the trigger.

I was startled by the click of the gun, but no bullet was expelled.   Like a derailed freight train, gut wrenching grief gripped me and I felt intense remorse for wanting to end my life.   I threw the gun back in the drawer and ran to my room, locked the door behind me, and melted into a puddle of tears on my bed.

"Oh God, I'm so sorry! What was I thinking? I'm so so so stupid and could have killed myself! Oh God, Oh God, please forgive me!"

Hours later I woke up to my mom shaking me and hysterically shouting, "Angie! Angie! Wake up!"   I hadn't heard her frantically pounding on the door.

When I finally came out of the emotional coma, she tightly wrapped her arms around me and I could hear her sobbing, "I thought you were dead! Oh God, I thought you were dead! My baby, my baby, I thought you were dead!"

In that moment, I welcomed her embrace and wept uncontrollably, my body shaking and gasping for air between the deep moans of grief and regret. Oh how my heart hurts for those who have lost someone to suicide, especially a child.

The Invisible Enemy

Please hear me as I share this important insight. There is a real dark force in this world that speaks to our spirit in the deep shadows of our pain. Agents of this demonic realm do all they can to drown out the still small voice of God, leading people down paths of destruction, addiction, heartbreak, isolation and death.

Hurting kids are such an easy target.

All those disparaging thoughts I was having, that seemed to come from nowhere, were actually from demonic spirits attempting to push me into the pit of despair. Without information about this invisible realm, many are left believing these dark thoughts are their own, which often brings even more condemnation, shame, and guilt.

One trick the demons like to play is to convince you that even having the thought means you have sinned, which is simply not true. However, once you partner with the thought, accept it as your own and act on it, that is when sin is formed.

In being transparent about the gruesome details of my own story, I hope to bring awareness to this dangerous unseen realm and the nature of our invisible enemy who prowls around like a lion, seeking someone to devour.

Satan's kingdom is very real, and he is hell bent on destroying mankind, *especially* those who have accepted Christ as their Savior, since they carry the ultimate power to defeat his evil plots.

Make it a point today, right now, to cry out to Jesus. Not just to know about him intellectually, but to know him relationally. Jesus is the only authority greater than Satan. And when we invite him as Lord over our lives, we take our position over Satan.

Here's that simple prayer given to me at nine years old:

God, I'm a sinner and need you to save me. I believe you sent Jesus to pay the price for my wrongdoings with his death on the cross, and that you raised him back to life three days later. I profess Jesus Christ is Lord and receive the power of the Holy Spirit to fill me so I can live a life worthy of my calling. In Jesus name I pray. Amen.

If Jesus was willing to save a wretch like me, he will absolutely do the same for you. Nothing is too hard for God! You are valuable and worth saving!

I invite you to stand on my experiences and learn what took me more than three decades to understand —Jesus is the only way to true peace and freedom. Don't wait another second because this life is but a vapor, gone in a flash. Your transformation is meant to inspire and change someone else's life, in addition to your own!

Jesus promises that if you seek him with your whole heart, you will find him. He loves to reveal himself to those who diligently search for him, no matter what darkness you're living through right now. And believe me, his unconditional love is so worth the effort.

Why continue to go through the same cycles of pain and regret when there is another way?

Personal Reflections

***

For he satisfies the longing soul, and the hungry soul he fills with good things.

Psalm 107:9 ESV

Chapter 4: Shallow Soil

When you're operating with a distorted self-image that stems from enduring traumatic and painful events, it dramatically affects the choices you make in life.

While I do not mean to discount the amazingly beautiful experiences I've had, namely the blessings of my three children, I've had to overcome some tremendous hardships because of the choices *I* made, which led down a path of brokenness and abusive relationships, including the relationship with myself.

The key to my personal transformation came when I resolved to question what *I* was doing to invite or allow these type of behaviors to affect my life, instead of merely submitting to the will of those who used me as a means to satisfy their own desires.

It would take the onset of my second divorce from a violent man to finally call attention to this urgent quest of evaluating the condition of my own heart.

Superficial Connections

All throughout high school and college, I entered into intimate relationships on the primary basis of sex. And while they typically morphed into longer term commitments, bypassing the all-important courtship process eventually led to unfulfilled desires.

When the seed of a relationship is planted in the shallow soil of the physical body, instead of first digging down deeper into the soul (mind, will, and emotions), the seed tends to dry up or get washed away in the storms of life because it doesn't root down deep enough. That's why it's possible to go through the motions of sex, but be emotionally disengaged.

However, when you are soulfully engaged with your partner, sex becomes a celebration of closeness, not a means to becoming close. Love must be rooted beyond the mere physical aspect in order to flourish through our thoughts, language, and actions towards the other person.

One of the greatest treasures you have to offer is to reserve the purity of your body for your spouse. That is how God designed us, to be fully committed to someone, not just sexually.

Since the separation from my second husband in 2013, I have resolved to live a life of celibacy. If I am meant to be married again one day, it will be to a man who chases after Jesus and values the reservation of sex for the marriage bed.

If we are unable to sustain our connection on a soul and spiritual level, then how will our relationship survive through the perils of old age when the strength of our bodies is diminished?

True Acceptance

Building a relationship with God has been more than enough to satisfy my soul in a way that I no longer give thought to seeking sexual gratification. His love is that powerful! That's saying a lot coming from a gal who formed ideas of her worth around sex at the age of nine.

My worth is now rooted in how God sees me, which goes beyond the soul level and is rooted in the core of my spirit. It took a long time to get here though and I'm continually being purged of the negative mindsets of my old nature.

Once you accept Jesus Christ as your Savior, God's Holy Spirit comes to take up residence in your innermost cavity, transforming you from a 2-dimensional being (body and soul) into a 3-dimensional being (body, soul, and spirit). Lasting transformation only comes from the inside out, starting within the spirit, then the soul (mind, will, emotions), and finally in the physical body.

For example, if you have a negative view of your body, diet and training will only take you so far. If your physical appearance becomes the basis of your self-worth, then it starves your soul of the nourishment it desires. Engaging in soul-enhancing activities will naturally affect how you see yourself physically.

It is said that the eyes are the windows to the soul. If you see yourself through dark or critical lenses, then that's an indication of a negative mindset that needs to be removed from your soul. No amount of exercise can do that. It must come from the inside out, driven by the divine power source of God's Spirit at the center of your core.

Misguided Motives

I met my first husband in college, at the peak of my physical prowess. No longer was I the skinny girl absent of the sexy curves I so longed for in high school. I had fully blossomed into womanhood, feeling affirmed through the modeling agencies who touted my toned abs and slender, yet muscular, legs. Finally, I began to feel empowered in my self-image at the age of 19.

We fell in love quickly. He made me feel valued with his admiration of my body and career mindedness. He also had a chivalrous way about him, which fed the deep need in my soul to feel protected and loved by a man.

About six months into our relationship, we had an alcohol induced argument about something and he threatened to break it off with me. I don't recall the context of the argument, but I remember feeling completely devastated at the thought of losing him.

So much of my identity was wrapped up in our relationship. It seemed he was able to so easily discard me, which sent me right back to the memories of being dumped by my first boyfriend.

In a panic, I literally begged him not to leave, and he finally agreed. We eventually worked everything out, but that seed of doubt and rejection had been planted.

In the beginning of our second year dating, he was drafted into the minor leagues for the Oakland A's baseball team. And although he moved to Oregon, we continued dating long distance, while I poured myself into school and work. We dreamed of him making it to the big league and living an extravagant lifestyle together.

Shortly after he was passed over for advancement by a less qualified player, he decided to leave the program. His ego had been badly damaged by the rejection. The organization simply wanted to further their investment in the other guy, regardless of how he ranked in skill, because he had been drafted in a higher round.

While he insisted his decision was motivated by his deep longing to be with me again, I sensed it was more of an issue with pride. You see, he had grown up as a sports star in his hometown, due to his own talents, as well as the celebrity status of his step-dad.

Being rejected and not being able to leverage the family status was simply not in his wheelhouse.

While we grew closer with his return, subconsciously I felt unsteady in his commitment to me. Something had changed in him, like he had lost a big part of his identity and I worried he would resent me for leaving his love of baseball.

As we neared the two year mark of our courtship, I began to drop hints about marriage. Then the subtle hints turned into full on pressure, until he finally proposed.

I don't doubt he loved me, but my insecurities robbed us both of the joyful surprise that should accompany a wedding proposal. In essence, I was more motivated by him proving his commitment to me than addressing any issues of false security.

Immediately after graduating college, we celebrated with a lavish wedding. Life seemed to be going perfectly for awhile. We moved from Tennessee to a northern suburb of Illinois. While I quickly found my way into a promising career, he struggled to find lasting enjoyment in what he did.

Wounded Souls

Moving back near all his family and friends seemed to add pressure on him to live up to a celebrity standard. It was during our first month of marriage that he began to make degrading comments about me in front of his friends. It was so contrary to our life together back in TN.

Instead of standing up for myself, I took on the passive role of a victim and my insecurities grew like wildfire. We toggled back and forth between fighting and making up, seeming to lose our footing in resolving the ongoing conflict.

The heavy consumption of alcohol, recreational drugs, and fatty foods became the comfort of our partying lifestyle, which led to burnout and boredom in our relationship. The perfect body he so cherished about me in college seemed to become the vocalized concern of his dissatisfaction in our relationship.

For the next several years, I yearned to attain perfection because I believed that's what it would take to regain his interest. My motivations were based on satisfying his view of me, instead of caring for my own soul.

Because I had never dealt with the brokenness of the sexual assault at age nine, my priorities in life were totally skewed and determined from the outside-in, instead of from the inside-out.

Eventually, after repeated failures to maintain the model figure of those college years, I convinced myself that I was repulsive and began to avoid sex with my husband, especially in the light.

To others, we were often called the perfect couple, but we were merely putting on our fake smiles to gain admiration from the outside world. All the while, our relationship was quickly deteriorating behind the scenes.

Gradually, our focus shifted to accumulating more stuff, going on vacations, and throwing the best parties. This landed us deeper into debt, which only forced us to run faster on the hamster wheel to make money so we could keep up the facade of a successful lifestyle. Add multiple DUIs, job loss, the responsibility of raising kids, coupled with dual infidelity, and you have the perfect recipe for hostile disagreements.

My first husband had his own brokenness to manage, as we all do, which spiraled into alcohol-induced rages that ultimately led to physical and emotional abuse. To rekindle our romance, he insisted we needed to spice things up by adding another sex partner into the mix. That shift in him completely devastated me.

He might as well have taken a dagger to my already frail heart. However, instead of working through things with him, I turned to accepting comfort outside the sanctity of our marriage. Neither of us were innocent bystanders in the desecration of our vows.

Death Wish

Sometime between 2005-2006 when my marriage hit an all time low, I received a message that my father Jack was trying to reach me. For days I stewed over what he possibly had to say to me after what he did. I was so livid, my whole body was like a burning inferno.

I had already rehearsed in my mind how the conversation would go before I called him back, determined to inflict as much punishment as I could with my words.

When he answered the phone, I demanded to know why he was contacting me. He attempted to make small talk, commenting on how he heard I had twins. He himself is a twin, so naturally this would be a point of connection in a normal conversation.

However, I unleashed a furry of assaulting words back on him. I made it very clear that I wanted absolutely nothing to do with him, stooping as low as to saying he was dead to me.

Oh he tried to convince me he was a changed man, claiming he had gotten right with God and all. Well, having no framework for what that actually meant, I completely dismissed it as a copout. Honestly, even if he had tried to apologize to me, I was in no state of mind to accept it into my heart. I abruptly hung up and broke down in tears.

I had done what I intended to do and gave him the greatest verbal lashing of my lifetime. *So why did I feel like something had just died inside of me?* Actually, I felt worse than before the call— treacherously and utterly disgusted with my response, but I had no healthy outlet to process those deep-seeded emotions.

Many have said that bitterness is like you drinking poison and waiting for the other person to die. Well, I had taken a massive gulp of that bitter poison and could feel myself slowly dying inside.

I later learned that forgiveness is an integral part of healing. Without it, there is no way to break your soul free from the chains of darkness.

Only by the strength of God's Spirit can we truly forgive horrendous acts done against us. The bitterness I held towards my father would leave my soul shattered for another debilitating ten years, causing even more destruction to pile up against me.

Downward Spiral

After an intense physical attack, at the hands of my inebriated husband, I decided to file for divorce. Overcome by fear, I had lost the strength to fight for our marriage any longer, even as he begged me to stay and help him overcome his addiction to alcohol. It seemed easier to walk away than to deal with the mess.

Over the next year, I sought fulfillment in all the wrong places. I quickly returned to using my body as a means of attracting attention, jumping from one volatile relationship to the next.

I sank deeper into depression, until I had finally fallen into the same trap of addiction, scoring a DUI on my record and a stern warning from my parents that I had better shape up.

I eventually left a high paying job because I had become entangled in an adulterous relationship with a member of management and could no longer bear the guilt and shame that weighed on me. I jumped from job to job seeking a way to fill the emptiness inside, but nothing satisfied the deep hunger for love.

Having been manipulated and hurt by so many men, I began having thoughts of dating women. Again these thoughts seemed to bombard me from the outside. Suddenly, as soon as I entertained the thought, it was like an invisible sign illuminated over my head.

I was literally sitting at home contemplating the idea of dating women, and within an hour, a female friend called and confessed she couldn't help her attraction to me. I wasn't ready to explore at that point, and was really freaked out by how the thoughts had so quickly manifested.

Over the next few days, I received social media messages from strange women who expressed their interest in dating. That had never happened before! Random women began approaching me for my number when I'd go out. "What was going on?" I thought.

For several weeks I carried on a conversation with one of the gals, but was upfront about my hesitation to pursue a relationship. In that timeframe, I began having sexual dreams about being with women. It was like something was trying to tell me this was the path to fulfillment, but inside it just felt wrong, so I started pushing the thoughts away and broke off the connection with this woman.

Even as my relationships with men ended, for various and unimportant reasons, I would long for someone to just call me to stroke my wounded ego. Suddenly and on multiple occasions, some guy I had met at a party, or an old boyfriend would call just as I was having these thoughts.

With that, I really began to question the power of my thoughts. I had heard of people being psychic, and I was beginning to wonder if I had that same ability.

That began my exploration into supernatural phenomenon, which opened up a whole new world. My ex-husband and I had always been fascinated with stories of alien and ghost encounters, and had even dabbled with the Ouija Board game, but nothing could prepare me for what would happen next.

I didn't know it at the time, but all these incidents were being orchestrated by demonic influences. I began treading on dangerous ground, and in my misguided search for fulfillment, I had naively opened doors to the occult.

Personal Reflections

Personal Reflections

*✲✲

Your words are so powerful that they will kill or give life, and the talkative person will reap the consequences.

Proverbs 18:21 TPT

Chapter 5: Dangerous Doors

In early 2010, three and a half years after separating from my ex-husband, my eyes were opened to the path of destruction that lay ahead of me if I continued to burn the candle at both ends.

I don't remember exactly what it was that sparked the change in perspective, other than I just felt a strong internal warning. It was as if I heard a whisper saying, *"Ok, that's enough. You're killing yourself!"*

That's when I started searching for balance and meaning in my life again. I had finally exhausted the self sabotaging ways of coping with the pain of losing my marriage. It was at that time I began to break connections with the bad influences and dedicated myself to rebuilding my life. I started my own brokerage business and poured myself into building a client portfolio.

I was making better choices and began enjoying quiet reflective time. I sought counseling through a holistic doctor and surrounded myself with positive personalities. She confirmed that the extreme physical and emotional stress of the volatile twin pregnancy, along with the damaging circumstances of my marriage, sparked the battle with Graves' Disease.

"If you continue to put off treatment of the disease, you will most likely die of heart failure," she warned. At 38 years old, my resting heart rate soared well over 100 beats per minute. Any amount of light exercise completely taxed my breathing, and I swung from hyperactivity to extreme fatigue.

On top of it all, I had taken up cigarette smoking as a way to deal with anxiety during the months leading up to the separation, which taxed my heart even more. Simply put, I was a wreck. It was time to give my body the rest and regeneration it so craved.

Power Sources

Some of the other single women I had known began to invite me into some new age practices. I bought tarot cards, visited a psychic medium, and began meditating on the characteristics of my ideal mate. I was told, if I spoke my desires out to the "universe," my perfect mate would be drawn to me.

Interestingly, I sort of half-heartedly joked about being done with the bar scene and how I would likely marry the next guy I dated. Little did I realize the power those spoken words carried out into the spiritual realm.

Much later in my faith journey, I came to understand that there are only two kingdoms on earth —God's and Satan's. God's is the ruling authority over all, however, he grants dominion of the earth to mankind. And in his rebellion against God, Satan was cast down to earth. Satan still has power, but lacks authority on earth. It is our partnership with Satan's mindset (sin) that allows him to usurp our authority. And it is our partnership with God's kingdom that subdues the evil.

In a vision, God illustrated the power of spoken words. I saw two beings in front of me. I understood one to be an angel and one to be a demon. When I chose to speak blessings and kind words, I saw the words form into an assignment that went to the angel. When I spoke curses, or negative words, the assignment went to the demon and turned into a chain link that could be used to bind someone, or even myself.

Without knowing, we often speak word curses over ourselves and people we love. Have you ever said, "I'm so stupid!" when you made a mistake? Or perhaps you've complained about never having enough money. You are actually cursing yourself! The Bible says we have the power to bless or to curse with our words. *Are you employing angels or demons with your speech?*

Strange things began to happen around the house. Lights would flicker on and off as I entered a room, doors would randomly open and shut, and I could actually hear audible voices speaking when no one was around. *Was I going crazy?*

I lived in a large house that had significant space between neighbors, but I had an eery sense I was being watched. I'd experience breezes while inside the house, and there were no open windows or vents blowing near me. I couldn't make sense of it all. *Did ghosts suddenly move into the house?*

I had always been creeped out by the first floor of the tri-level house, which was my ex-husband's man cave when he lived there. Shortly after we had moved into the home, we would be hanging out on the first level and my skin would crawl. The room was very spacious, but it gave me such a claustrophobic feeling, like I was suffocating. I hadn't recalled ever feeling that way before.

Cursed

Within the first months of owning the home, my husband and I had heard rumors that a young Navy recruit had gone awol and the original owners of the house had taken him in. It was said that once he was inside, they sodomized and tortured him before eventually killing him.

Interestingly, during a landscape project, we found a heavy chain with a padlock around the base of a tree, and a military uniform buried deep underground. It really creeped us out, but we brushed it off and turned it into a great ghost story at parties.

The lady who sold the house to us also jokingly warned that it was cursed, stating that everyone who lived there either separated or divorced within the first year of moving in, including her and her husband. We chalked it up to folklore and thought nothing more about it because we absolutely loved the house.

I'll have you know, we separated exactly one year after moving in—almost to the day! Coincidence? After studying the Bible, I can emphatically say that the house was truly cursed with demonic activity, and without the protection of Jesus, we were absolutely defenseless against it sabotaging our marriage.

Remembering back to the times with my husband in the man cave, and now experiencing this strange phenomenon as a single woman in the house, I decided it would be best to keep things cordial with the ghostly spirit that was in the house.

So I started saying hello when strange things happened and casually announced the spirit was welcome as long as it didn't hurt anyone. I didn't know what else to do. Nor did I understand the spiritual consequences of those statements.

I was suddenly more engaged with watching ghost stories on TV, in order to learn how to deal with what was happening. That only made things worse because I was scared out of my wits to be alone in the house. Plus it seemed to open a portal of more strange phenomenon.

I could keep myself pretty busy when my kids were there, but when they were gone to their dad's, I dreaded being alone, so I did what most people do to feel protected—I bought a massive dog!

This was no ordinary dog though. Roxie was a mix between an English Mastiff and an Irish Wolfhound, and bred to be the largest dog in the world.   Before she was a year old, she weighed a whopping 100 pounds!

Needless to say, she was way too much dog for me and she totally destroyed the house without enough exercise. *What was I thinking trying to add a small horse-sized dog to the mix, when I so needed to destress my life?* That was a hard lesson learned. Plus I really didn't feel any safer. You can't fight a spiritual battle with human weapons.

Cosmic Set-up

Remember that joke about marrying the next guy I dated? Well, that turned out to be true. I met my second husband online within a week of posting my profile.

There was something different about him. He wasn't like any of the other guys I dated. He was a muscle head who drove a Harley, smoked cigars, and was all tatted up. I typically dated athletes or business guys up to that point.

He came on really strong, but in a strangely endearing way. Unlike previous relationships, I had committed to hold off on sex until I determined our emotional compatibility. I was once again ready for a serious relationship and didn't want to complicate things with sex too soon. Reluctantly, he agreed, so it left more time for conversation.

We spent hours on the phone, and by the third date, he said he loved me and was going to marry me. I was taken aback and super skeptical at first, but didn't want to close my heart to any "fairytale" opportunities.

He pursued me with fervor, treating me like royalty and wooing me through unending flattery. It was like drenching my dry soul with cool refreshing water after a long trip in the desert heat.

Our relationship progressed at supersonic speed, and within 4-5 months, he moved into the house. Oddly enough, I also started having disturbing dreams of bugs and spiders crawling on me or the walls after he moved in. I'd wake up desperate to get them off of me.

I realize now, they were warnings of what I was partnering with— indications of mind control spirits related to witchcraft, and living in sin against the sanctity of marriage.

Looking back, I also recognize there were some serious red flags with his possessive behaviors, but I chose to ignore them. I wanted to remain open to love and was willing to sacrifice a little personal space for it. You see, when your soul is wounded, even the wrong attention can be more appealing than no attention. Plus, I had acquired that desire to love bullies back in childhood.

The ghostly activity also heightened after he moved in. While watching a movie together one evening, the volume on the TV shot way up. We looked to see if the remote was underneath us. Then gasped as I pointed to the remote positioned on the arm of the love seat about three feet away from us. It was the only volume control for the TV. We were both freaked out!

One night, he had gotten up to use the bathroom and heard a man laughing. He quickly rushed in to find me sound asleep. It was clearly a man's voice and not one I could have faked. He looked outside the windows, and there was no one around, which would have been highly unlikely anyway.

There were many times we'd arrive back at the house and could smell marijuana concentrated in the foyer. It wasn't ours—besides, smoke rises and doesn't remain in one concentrated spot like this did.

It became a joke, as we left the house, to ask the ghost to keep an eye on things.

Right on cue, our relationship started to deteriorate in sync with the house's history of the one year curse. He moved out, but was persistent in making things work, claiming that we needed a fresh start in our own place. *"Maybe it is just the house,"* I thought.

We moved into a different place shortly thereafter and although volatile at times, he was so committed to being together, treating me like his beautiful queen, which was so different from my first husband, who found ways to escape or divide our family time.

Another year later, I married my second husband— despite my internal warnings and the cautionary advice of a close friend. That's when the result of my choices caused life to take on another drastic and scary turn.

Personal Reflections

***

But if we confess our sins to him, he is faithful and just to forgive us our sins and to cleanse us from all wickedness.

1 John 1:9 NLT

Chapter 6: Poor Patterns

My second husband and I both desired to have a child, which was at the core of why we decided to get married in the first place. Our daughter, who was conceived on our honeymoon, was his first child, and my third.

Interestingly, in both of my pregnancies, I conceived right away. With my first husband, I knew we were having twins long before the doctor confirmed it. And with my second husband, I openly expressed the deep desire to have a girl. God would continue to reveal to me much later in my journey with Him, that there is tremendous power in the words we speak, especially by those who carry his Holy Spirit.

Throughout the courtship with my second husband, our limited intimate bedroom affairs seemed awkwardly disconnected. However, since most of my previous partnerships had evolved around the physical connection, I chose to set aside this desire, in favor of companionship.

It's not that I didn't love my second husband, but we seemed far more focused on supporting and encouraging one another. Rarely did we share the deep conversations of life or express the overwhelming desire to be physically intimate with one another. It seemed we both just wanted the comfort of knowing there was someone else to walk with through life.

I later discovered that the suppression of an intimate physical connection in marriage was not only ungodly, but it also weakened our ability to reconcile differences. Sexual intimacy between husband and wife is actually encouraged by God—so that Satan won't be able to cause division.

Skewed Perspectives

Part of the initial attraction to my second husband was his profession of faith. I had never been involved with anyone who practiced religion, on any regular sort of basis, and it fascinated me.

As part of the condition for getting married in his church, I was required to convert to Greek Orthodoxy. Having no formal religious upbringing, and never having read the Bible, I was quite excited to learn more about God.

However, what I learned in those classes only confused my understanding of God, and seemed contradictory to my very limited experience in childhood. There seemed to be a stricter view of God's expectations in the Greek Orthodox faith.

I also questioned why God would care about things like women not wearing pants, crossing their legs during service, or going beyond certain areas of the priestly quarters.

Did God place greater importance on men? And why did you have to do the sign of the cross every time the Trinity was mentioned, which was more than a few dozen times in service?

All these rules seemed so distracting! These questions were quickly glossed over or met with vague answers during class. By the end of the course, I believe the teachers were quite ready for me to move on.

Seeking knowledge and understanding has always been a part of my internal wiring—admittedly to the point of annoyance for some adults and teachers over the course of my life, especially when they were unable to sufficiently satisfy my curiosity.

My internal senses also kept alerting me with a feeling that something just wasn't adding up in their views of God. But I brushed it all aside because I wanted to make a good impression and not flunk out of the course—ultimately derailing our marriage plans.

What did I know anyway? All these guys had years of experience in the church and theology degrees to back up their Bible knowledge credentials. I had never even read the Bible so I took their word for it.

During the conversion ceremony, as well as later in the baptism of our daughter, I was so overwhelmed with tears—to the point of the heaving chest ugly cry!

It was embarrassing because I couldn't understand why I was crying so much. I wasn't sad. In fact, I was elated and felt there was a beautiful holiness in what we were doing.

In hind site, I realize it was the presence of God causing that response. Even now as I think about God's presence, tears of joy and gratitude well up in my eyes!

In my faith journey, I've noticed many church goers are caught in the cycle of routine, or trying so hard to earn God's acceptance. Often they are carrying the attitude that God is just waiting for them to step out of line so he can punish them. That is not the God of love who created mankind and invites them into a personal relationship with Jesus.

If God is looking for reasons to punish us, then why would He send Jesus, whom He loved, in order to save us? How could I have felt such overwhelming love and acceptance when inviting Jesus into my heart at nine years old?

I had no previous knowledge of God, other than what the preacher spoke about that day at Terry's church—that Jesus loved me unconditionally and wanted to dwell within me, in order to impart His goodness in and through me. That is the true Gospel message in a nutshell!

As we began attending church more regularly, I found myself becoming so annoyed with the rules and not wanting to go. I desired to know more about God, but it felt like work without any reward. Eventually we stopped going, but the nagging tug of curiosity still beckoned me to seek more.

Our neighbors had invited us to the local non-denominational church, but one of the rules of the Greek Orthodox faith was you had to remain within that denomination, so we passed on the invitation.

Control

We all need to experience God's unconditional love at the center of our lives before we can truly give and receive love to the world around us. I hadn't quite tapped into God's love at this juncture in my life, so when my second husband's behavior began to turn emotionally abusive, it drudged up the past wounds and insecurities of my soul.

We attempted counseling. However, what I learned is that forgiveness can be one-sided, but reconciliation requires both parties. It was clear to me that my husband's intentions were not set on reconciling, but on control—and ultimately dominating me at all cost. Controlling behaviors tend to be rooted in the fear of inadequacies, and we can all exercise varying levels of it.

Things between us began to quickly unravel at the progression of the pregnancy. I felt like he treated me more as a "vessel for his" child than his wife. During a disagreement, I recall him saying I didn't know 90% of who he actually was. It wasn't until we were going through the divorce a few months later that I discovered the full extent of that comment. He had an extensive violent past, especially towards women.

I had ignored the multiple warnings signs and hadn't invested enough time in getting to know him on a deep and intimate level before marriage. As I look back now, through the eyes of a healed soul, I can clearly see I had defiled the sanctity of marriage and was suffering the horrific consequences of that choice. Plus it goes without saying, he was battling with his own childhood wounds.

Prison of Offense

Pastor Steven Furtick of Elevation Church preached a sermon on the "Prison of Offense." His message effectively demonstrates how Satan magnifies small offenses to divide relationships. If the "of-fense" is not dealt with swiftly, then it causes "a-fence" to come between people. I highly encourage you to check out the message.

Think about it—fences are meant to keep people in or out, depending on how you look at it. While my second husband used controlling behaviors to keep me fenced in the relationship, I erected my own fence to push him out. Neither is right, and both are rooted in the fear of being rejected.

Only love can defend against offense.

In my past, I focused on the unfair actions of my abusers, which caused me to see things from a limited and wounded perspective, placing most of the blame on the other person. I realize now that I wasn't ready to face what needed to be healed within me—a brokenness in my own soul that caused me to remain trapped in a victim mentality. In this writing assignment, I have chosen instead to look at how my own fear-based choices led me right into the snare of destruction. It is not my objective to minimize the pain of traumatic experiences for anyone who has been unjustly victimized. Rather, I want to take us beyond hiding in the darkened areas of our wounded souls, and out into the healing light of true freedom!

Cycle Interruption

Because the relationship with my second husband was based more on shallow companionship, instead of being deeply rooted in intimacy and knowledge of one another, we became easily offended when the other didn't perform to our standards, whether those standards were realistic or not. Safe emotional boundaries were crossed, often unintentionally, because we didn't have a full understanding of where the lines were.

As I mentioned before, there's a saying that "hurt people hurt other people." It's meant to give us a different perspective beyond our own, and to understand the basis for why people resort to abusive behaviors. I'm a firm believer that most abusers were once, and perhaps still are, victims of abuse themselves.

Remember those bullies back in childhood? They were often suffering from older family members picking on them. My second husband had experienced intense bullying from family members growing up, which had a significant impact on how he saw himself and, ultimately, how he treated others.

With this in mind, I don't want to give the impression that I am minimizing abusive behavior as we move forward. There absolutely should be measures of accountability for injustice. Without accountability, most abusers will likely never feel the need to get into a position of humility before God. Accountability is a key element in transformation.

However, it's also important that abusers come to know the beautiful gift of grace that God pours out on those who turn to Him in repentance for their wicked choices. He is so merciful and looks for every opportunity to withhold judgement, no matter what you have done. I once heard the Lord say that the punishment is lessened for those who come forth with admission.

So while the repentant one may be required to still face the consequences of their actions, the tremendous burden of the soul is lifted by the grace of God. There is nowhere Jesus won't go to meet you, whether on the street corner, in the dark alleys, or in a prison cell. Better to save your soul and start living in right standing with God, than to proceed in wickedness and be eternally damned.

You must know that God does not seek out perfect people to work through—quite the contrary! He seeks to reveal Himself through weak and broken vessels who are surrendered to Him. Nothing is impossible for God.

Consider this—Albert Einstein is famously quoted as saying, "Insanity is doing the same thing over and over again, but expecting different results." What are the negative cycles in your life that you'd like to see changed? Perhaps it's poverty, addiction, sexual perversion, fear, pride, greed, or whatever else steals your peace and joy.

The only way to break the cycle permanently, is to eliminate the wounds and lies in your soul that feed the flies. God's Spirit is more than willing to bring his healing light into those darkened areas of your soul, but it will require you to trust him.

Personal Reflections

Personal Reflections

***

God is love.

1 John 4:16 NIV

Chapter 7: Holiness Highway

God is not looking for robots to obey Him. He created us with the free will to choose. The wickedness and destruction that we see in the world today is the result of mankind's choices to partner with evil motives. God owns the whole universe, but He gave mankind dominion over the earth.

If we choose to partner with Jesus, not only will we be filled with his unconditional love, he will also simultaneously lead us in the eradication of evil. You can either partner with God, or ignore him. The choice is yours.

In my case, I committed to seeking God shortly after the divorce proceedings began with my second husband, by attending that local non-denominational church with our neighbors. I didn't want to go back to the Greek Orthodox church because it lacked that loving feeling I had experienced in childhood. Plus, something just felt off with it.

I made a choice to attend the local church every week. Like milk to a newborn baby, I felt nourished by the encouraging messages. Eventually, my hunger for more grew and I began devouring online past sermons on a daily basis. When those ran out, I began attending other churches throughout the week and listening to respected teachers online.

Feeding on God gave me such a sense of empowerment over my circumstances!

About seven months into the journey, a massive wave of paranoia suddenly came over me. For weeks my thoughts were consumed by the fear of dying at the hands of my estranged husband. We were in the middle of the divorce proceedings and his behavior had grown even more erratic.

I discovered much later that during this time, he had knowledge of the completed custody investigation recommending me as the sole custodian of our daughter, which didn't get reported to me until more than a month later, due to some mix up with the email distribution.

You see, he had made false accusations against me to authorities and in court, so until a custody investigation was complete, we had to remain living together. This gave him a sense of control over the situation, and ultimately over me.

Abuse is modeled around one person maintaining power and control over another. It's most often when the abuser's position of power and control is challenged, that the worst damage is inflicted on the victim.

According to national statistics, <u>75% of domestic violence victims are murdered as they attempt to leave their abusive partner.</u> My exit door had finally opened, and I believe the loss of control my second husband would have over our daughter and I absolutely infuriated him.

While I have no physical proof of this claim, I believe he was actually contemplating poisoning me. Like the inner knowings and warnings I had felt since that childhood touch from God, it was like I could read his thoughts.

I didn't have knowledge of it at that point in my life, but Jesus read the thoughts of others, and since I was partnering with Holy Spirit, that meant he could reveal their thoughts to me as well, when he so chose.

My husband's history of extreme and repeated violence against women, along with the obvious loss of control that would come with physical separation, certainly supported a motive for murder.

Fountain of Love

It was in that moment of realization that I angrily cried out to God, "If this is how you want to take me, then so be it! Just do it already because I can't take this anymore! But if you're real, then I need you to show up and show me that you're real and HELP ME!"

In a flash, I felt an invisible presence come over me. It was so powerful that it knocked me down on my knees. I saw nothing with my eyes, but felt wave after wave of liquid love pouring all over my body. The sheer delight caused my body to tremble uncontrollably. Suddenly I envisioned myself as a glorious fountain with the water gushing up from inside my core, then covering over me like a refreshing waterfall.

The Creator of the universe had personally and powerfully revealed himself to me! I don't recall how long the encounter lasted, but I was hooked and had to have MORE of his magnificent presence. It felt a thousand times better than anything I had ever experienced in my life! Like a love-crazed junkie, I became utterly obsessed with chasing after Jesus.

His love washed away so many fears and insecurities that day, opening my eyes to a whole new world filled with beauty and hope. And just think, he is waiting to do the same thing for you or anyone else who chooses to seek after him wholeheartedly. Feeling the powerful love of Jesus Christ is worth more than any amount of fame and fortune!

You just can't make this stuff up! That's why many of his disciples endured severe torturing, even unto death, just to share his message of love with others. You must know this—Satan will stop at nothing to keep you from having a personal relationship with Jesus Christ.

Why do you think that is? Because once you finally grasp the magnitude of God's love for you, and the power that will pour forth from your inner core, you can sabotage Satan's plans for destruction! Ultimately, you become a weapon in God's hands to defeat evil.

Sacrifice

In order to give you the full picture, I would be remiss if I didn't tell you that having a personal relationship with Jesus Christ will require sacrifices.

Like any successful relationship, it requires loyalty, trust, time, and putting the other person's needs above your own. Just like when you get married, you give up dating anyone else.

As I began building my own relationship with Jesus, He spoke these words into my spirit:

"So it's not gonna be easy. It's gonna be really hard. And we're gonna have to work at this everyday, but I want to do that because I want you. I want all of you, forever, you and me, everyday."

That's a quote from The Notebook by Nicholas Sparks, and it beautifully illuminates God's desire to be in a relationship with us, every single day.

You will have to give up some of the comforts of this world. For many, that alone will be enough to keep them serving Satan's purposes. Unfortunately, anyone who chooses not to be in relationship with Jesus, automatically defaults to allying with the powers of darkness.

So while I had received the gift of the Holy Spirit at age nine, without pursuing a personal relationship with Jesus, I was actually serving Satan's purposes. I considered myself a pretty good person by most standards, but inside I was unfulfilled and just going through the motions. And with each trial that came, which is one of life's certainties, a little bit more of me died until I felt so empty inside.

If you're reading this book, then I imagine you are probably seeking more to life too. The great news is, once you reach the point of being emptied, that just leaves more room for Jesus to fill you up with His goodness!

Forgiveness

Another requirement of following Jesus is you will have to sacrifice being right all the time. After my love fountain encounter, one of the first requests Jesus asked of me was to forgive my estranged husband. At first I was like, *"What?! How is that even possible after all he's done?"* Again, that response came from a wounded soul.

As I began to investigate what it actually meant to forgive, the Lord gently reminded me of what he had endured on the cross to extend forgiveness to me. At that, I asked him to help soften my heart to see my husband the way he did. Releasing all that bitterness launched me into a profound journey of emotional healing.

Over the next year, I spent extensive time studying the Bible, building trust with Jesus, and developing a framework for the supernatural gifts of the Holy Spirit. I also embraced the challenge of a 40-day water only fast and my first Christian conference gathering, which led to the miraculous regeneration of my thyroid.

On the Throne

Following the spiritual fast and conference, I had a mind-blowing encounter with Jesus on his throne! During worship with a group of women, I was taken up into the spirit realm. My body remained in the room with the women, but my spirit was transported to another dimension. Now I am a very logical person, so this experience completely unraveled all my natural understanding.

The encounter began as I engaged with Jesus through my imagination. In this particular experience, I envisioned us riding horses together in the pasture of my childhood farmhouse. Suddenly, we began racing our horses. My breathing intensified and I actually felt like I was being submerged into the scene of my imagination.

In an instant, the scene went from racing horses to me standing before Jesus on his throne. He was about stage height, like you would see at a concert, but the platform was free floating in the air.

Standing alone in front of the stage, I was longing reaching my arms up to Jesus as he was speaking to a crowd of people further behind me.

I called out his name, and in that moment he reached his hand down towards mine and I was then instantaneously standing next to him before the throne. The seat of his throne reminded me of the white stone chair of the Lincoln Memorial in Washington DC.

Jesus looked so beautiful and radiated love from his very being. My heart was pounding with excitement just to be with him! Feeling like a giddy school girl, I stared intently at him, not sure what to do next.

Jesus then asked, "Would you like to sit with me on the throne?" as he gestured to the seat. *What?! Did I hear that right? Jesus wants ME to sit with HIM on the throne?*

"Yes, of course! I would love to!" I exclaimed in astonishment.

The moment we sat down together, our bodies immediately meshed into one person. It felt like the wind ruffling through my body and clothes, as if I was standing over an air vent.

Amazingly, I was now looking out to the crowd through HIS eyes! It's almost indescribable to explain the closeness I felt with Jesus. He was in me and I was in him—there was not one iota of separation between us!

Looking out into the crowd, I saw men, women and children of all ages and nationalities. They were wearing bright white garments.

A handful of them towards the left side had a large beautiful heart on their garment. It was such a deep red color and looked alive, but in a truly artistic way.

Jesus waved my arm over the crowd and said, "These are all my children. Some of them are hurting because they are being tormented. You will bring knowledge to them on how to be set free."

How was this even possible? And why ME? You must have the wrong person God! These were the thoughts that began bouncing around my head.

It was about that time that I became aware of my physical body back in the earthly realm. It had been shaking uncontrollably and I felt self-conscious about what the other women were thinking.

As I attempted to rationalize the experience, I felt myself pulling out of the encounter. One of the gals there encouraged me to stay in the vision. She spoke as if she had experience with this before, so I felt like I could trust her.

She told me, "Jesus has a gift for you. One in each hand." I then found myself standing confidently at the edge of a high cliff, with my feet planted on a rock formation that jutted out over an immense valley below me.

In my left hand was a massive sword. I held it with such ease and was enamored with the shimmer of the blade reflecting in the sunlight. I was filled with an immense sense of power and authority holding the sword. This represented the Sword of the Spirit, or the Word of God.

Although I am right-handed, the sword was in my weaker left hand, yet I held it with strength. This represented my divine calling to carry forth the Word of God through teaching and preaching, not in my own strength, but by the power of God.

In my right hand I held a giant red flower that filled my entire palm. It had the appearance of a plush lotus flower, with delicate yet majestic and stately petals. I felt this represented the Word of God being spoken in love to the members of Christ's body, or the corporate Church.

After that encounter, I was filled with a greater desire to do all the same things as Jesus did, like healing the sick, casting out demons, raising the dead, walking on water and so much more. The Bible says those who believe in Him would do greater works than He did, as they are seated together with Him in heavenly places.

Demonic Legal Rights

For the two days leading up to the encounter, I had felt a strong urge to research demonic legal rights. I wanted to know why demons were able to torment people, especially God's people who were suppose to be set free from sin. It appeared to be directly related to the agreement a person had with sinful behaviors, which is primarily due to a lack of partnership with Holy Spirit.

I discovered that even faith filled, Jesus loving Christians can have demonic attachments and influences in their lives. While a Christian who has accepted Christ as their Savior cannot be possessed, there are varying levels of oppression that can occur, depending on the degree to which you allow Holy Spirit to lead you. This is the torment Jesus referred to in my vision.

In one of the accounts of the Bible, where Jesus healed a lame man, he told the individual to stop sinning or something worse may happen to them. This supports the theory that engagement with sinful choices can lead to affliction.

Purging in Partnership

Holy Spirit is given to believers to lead and guide them into all truths. Walking fully surrendered to and in partnership with Holy Spirit will not lead a person into sinful paths because the conviction of God's Spirit will redirect the individual. The word says, if you love him you'll obey his commands.

This revelation is what started me down the path of purging negative thought patterns that led to my own sinful behaviors, be it anger, fear, or whatever is contrary to God's peace and joy. I would sit quietly with the Lord, pen and paper in hand, ready to discuss what needed to be pruned within me.

I would start out by engaging my imagination to meet with Jesus in the garden of my soul. Really engaging the full senses by imagining the sights, sounds, smells, touch, and taste of things in my garden. There's no right or wrong answer. The key is to remain focused on and engage with Jesus through your imagination. As you engage with the Lord, he will reveal the wounds of your soul, in order to bring deliverance and healing.

Now invite Jesus into your garden and take note of his features and what he's wearing. Welcome him with a hug, wrapping your own arms around yourself to feel the embrace. Take note of what he says to you while you are hugging (I love this part!).

Remember, there is no set pattern for working with the Holy Spirit, but it often requires you to be in a place that is free from distractions. Take note of what you are seeing, sensing, or feeling.

Generally it is safe to go with the first thought or picture that comes to mind. Otherwise, we tend to rationalize the response and second guess what we are sensing.

Ultimately, it's more important to follow the leading of the Holy Spirit when working through issues. The questions and statements are meant to give you a framework until you are confident with Holy Spirit's leading. Jesus himself tells us it requires childlike faith to get into the Kingdom of Heaven. Imagination is a gift.

Also keep in mind that God often talks in pictures. One time I was working through an issue of fear and the Lord gave me a picture of an armadillo when I asked what truth he wanted to share with me. What did that mean?

I quickly looked up the description of an armadillo online and found that it is nicknamed "little armored one." That certainly answered my desire to feel protected and safe! Allow yourself to be creative.

The following guide is also provided in the back of the book for quick reference, along with personal journaling pages.

Suggested Prayer Guide

Step 1

Find a quiet place to spend time with the Lord to work through the wounds of your soul. You can spend as little or as much time as you would like, so go at your own pace.

Step 2

Journal what the Lord shares with you. This will keep you on task, as well as honor the Lord by recording His words to you. Take note of what you see, sense, or hear.

Step 3

Commit to meet with the Lord on a regular basis. He looks forward to your time together and has much to reveal!

The following questions are intended to get you started, so again, be open to the Holy Spirit's leading.

- *What is in my garden that doesn't belong?*

- *What issue in my life does this represent? (Sinful behavior, issue, etc...)*

- *What lie am I believing about myself with this issue?*

- *When was this lie first planted in my soul?*

- *Repent for believing the lie and ask God to cleanse you of the unrighteous thinking with the blood of Jesus.*

- *Who do I need to forgive for believing this lie?*

- *Choose to forgive and repent to God for holding bitterness in your heart, then give Jesus permission to remove the unwanted item from your soul.*

- *What truth do you want me to receive about myself in this situation?*

- *Thank Jesus for the seed of truth and ask him to plant it into your garden.*

- *In exchange for all the pain and bitterness, what good gift do you want to give me to strengthen my defenses against any attempted return of these negative thoughts?*

- *Spend time thanking the Lord!*

Faith in Action

After the throne encounter and the months of concentrated purging partnership with Holy Spirit, praying for others and leading them into this path of holiness became a tremendous source of inspiration for me. I witnessed so many people healed and set free from torment by the power of Holy Spirit.

My spiritual maturity grew exponentially in such a short amount of time! A devoted man of God once shared these wise words, "The destination and pathway are the same for all Christians, but the pace and number of stops depends on our circumstances and relationship with the Lord." The hungrier you are for growth, the faster it tends to come.

The next step in my journey came in the Fall of 2015 when the Lord asked me to forgive my father Jack. I was so on fire with God's love, I agreed wholeheartedly.

During prayerful time with the Lord, He took me back to the memory of that night, while engaging the screen of my holy imagination. Again, that's where many of our encounters in the spirit realm occur—our imagination.

As I walked back through the memory, I watched it play from an outside perspective, like on a movie screen, allowing the deep-seeded fear that had planted itself in me 34 years prior, to rise up to the surface.

During this process, Jesus showed me where he had been standing that night, waiting for me to respond to his instructions to call out to him for help. Once I did, Jesus put his hand on my father's shoulder.

Ahhh—I now understood why my father had sat up so abruptly with that bizarre look on his face, before darting back to his bedroom! He had been convicted by God.

Jesus walked me through how to break agreements with the fear, bitterness, and sexual perversion that had marked me in the spirit realm. Those markers were actually evil spirits that drew the attention of other evil spirits to torment me. It finally made sense why I always felt like I had an "Easy Target" sign around my neck.

Think of it this way—it's like flies being drawn to rotting fruit. You can keep shooing the flies away, over and over again, only to have them return. It's only when we remove the rotting fruit in our souls that freedom from those pesky flies can be obtained. Appropriately enough, Satan is referred to as "Lord of the Flies," in the Bible.

We must surrender to Jesus and work with him to purify our souls. That's called sanctification. The gift of salvation, or forgiveness of sins, is instantaneous. However, sanctification is gradual and requires you to be in partnership with the Holy Spirit.

After working through the forgiveness of my father, I felt so much lighter and spent time worshipping and thanking Jesus! The whole process had been much easier than I had expected. However, the next step would prove to be a bit more difficult.

A few days later, Jesus asked me to call my father. I sort of stammered and protested a bit saying, "But Lord! Why do I have to call him?" He said, "You forgave him, right?" "Yes, Lord. I forgave him," I responded. Then Jesus said, "Trust me my love, I will be right beside you."

With that I chose to trust in the Lord, and began researching my father's contact information.

Personal Reflections

***

Within your heart you can make plans for your future, but the Lord chooses the steps you take to get there.

Proverbs 16:9 TPT

Chapter 8: Kingdom Come

It didn't take long to locate my father's contact information. *"Ok, here we go,"* I thought.

After spending time in prayer, I nervously dialed the number. My heart was pumping like a jackhammer in my chest, causing the phone to shake in my hands.

Prior to making the call, I attempted to play out every possible scenario of how the conversation might go, until the Lord finally said, "Don't worry child, I'll give you the words."

The call went to an general voicemail recording, so I had no real way of knowing I even had the right number. I don't remember exactly what I said as my head felt like it was spinning—probably from the elevated heart rate!

I managed to spit out something like, "Uh, hi. Uh, this is Angie. Um, your daughter. Um, you were, uh, married to my mom, Christie." Between stammers I was thinking, *What if he doesn't remember me?"* Of course he would remember me, duh! He had reached out to me back when I gave him that verbal lashing.

After leaving my phone number, I hung up and could hardly think of anything else. Questions began racing through my head, *"Would he call me back that night, or the next day?" "What if he doesn't want to talk to me? Was he even still alive?"*

He had called me within a couple days and left a short message, "Angie, this is your dad. Call me back." It took me another week to call him back— mostly due to fear related procrastination. I also really wanted to be alone when I talked with him, so it had to be a night that the kids were away.

As I dialed his number, I felt a bit calmer this time. After fumbling through the first few seconds, we actually had a surprisingly pleasant conversation! I started off by telling him I had found the love of Jesus, and since He had forgiven me of so much, I wanted to extend that same love and forgiveness to others. At that point, I half expected him to say, "Ok, good to know."

But instead, he gushed about how my phone call had been an answered prayer! He had also gotten right with God and wanted to make things right with me. He didn't say it, but I sensed that's what he was trying to do when he called me that last time. We talked about our families, and I was excited to hear about my other side of the family, which included more brothers, sisters, nieces and nephews.

We had many other pleasant discussions over the next several months. Each time, I wanted to bring up the incident, but couldn't bring myself to ask him about it. It needed to be just the right time. Later, I realized I had been longing for him to say those healing words of, "I'm sorry."

He had certainly implied he was sorry, but hearing the words brings healing on a whole other level. In any case, I was truly grateful we were both connected again—not only as father and daughter, but as members of God's family.

Inspiration

The reconciliation with my father opened my eyes to dream bigger with God! If He could forgive and transform a man who sexually assaulted his own daughter, then anything was possible! I couldn't help but share the news with my church family.

Like wildfire, good news like that spreads quickly! Several church leaders stopped me at different times to congratulate me and ask about the experience. One day, during a time of sharing testimonies, I briefly announced to the congregation what God had done between me and my father. Many agreed, it was truly a miracle!

It was more than a decade earlier, in my 30s, when I had confessed to my mom what had happened at my father's house that one summer. And the account of the event was conveyed to her through the utterance of a severely wounded soul, long before I began walking with Jesus.

So telling my mom that I had forgiven and reconnected with my biological father was much more difficult to do, and it lacked the celebratory response from her that came in sharing with Spirit-filled believers. She feared the change in him was untrustworthy. From the position of not knowing or recognizing God, I can see why fear would drive her reasoning.

It seems impossible to understand God's transforming power until you encounter his unconditional love and forgiveness for yourself. The spiritual truths of the Bible, such as forgiveness, seem foolish to those who do not have the Spirit of God within them because it is only in partnership with Holy Spirit that we are able to discern and understand.

Even for faithful believers, it's a continual surrender to forgive those who hurt you. Jesus said we are to forgive continually. He wouldn't ask us to do the impossible on our own. That's the reason why he gave us the precious gift of Holy Spirit as our counselor and teacher.

As Christians, we are commanded to forgive—it's not optional. That does not mean we don't maintain safe boundaries, but we must surrender the bitterness to God before it takes root in our hearts. He declares that vengeance is his.

My safe boundaries were about to be broadened.

Extending Borders

In the Summer of 2016, my new sister, Jessica, came to visit the kids and I in Chicago. We planned to meet at the Shedd Aquarium with all our children and her mom (my father's wife). The kids and I excitedly anticipated meeting this new side of our family, so when the day finally arrived, it felt like opening gifts on Christmas morning! We all bonded instantly and had such a wonderful time exploring the aquarium.

It is one of the most interesting experiences meeting a close family member for the first time as an adult. How you immediately begin taking note of the physical similarities and mannerisms between you. It completely fascinates me!

My father's wife is just the sweetest lady you could ever meet. She loves her family and is always giving her time sacrificially to help others. She has the kindest eyes and heart. It gave me great comfort knowing this was my father's wife. He sounded so gentle on the phone, and I wanted it to be true beyond our conversations.

Jessica shared how much our father and I sounded alike in the way we talked about God. That made me all the more excited to see him!

Later that year the Lord urged me to go deeper in reconciling the relationship and instructed me to plan a visit to see my father in person. While we were building our connection through phone conversations, seeing him in person would require some serious trust. Not because I feared he would hurt me again, but I felt anxious about how I would handle any awkwardness between us. *Should I stay with him or in a hotel? Should I take the kids or go alone?*

I felt it was best to go without the kids the first time, so he and I could spend time getting to know one another. Here I was going to meet my father after 34 years of being estranged, so it was likely there would be some tears involved, and I wanted to shield the kids from that.

Two's Company

While in a housing transition, I was staying with a friend and getting prepared for the trip. For some reason, I kept procrastinating, undecided if I should leave that day or the next morning. It was a bit of a last minute trip and I had to time everything just right in order to get back for the kids' return, but I didn't want to be too tired driving at night.

Interestingly, my friend's husband was relaxing in the back yard when he very clearly felt the Lord tell him that his wife needed to go with me on the trip. She had just arrived home after work and was looking forward to a relaxing weekend with her kids.

However, her husband was insistent that the Lord wanted her to go with me.

No wonder I had been procrastinating! We all prayed about it and each felt the Lord's approval for her to go with me. So with bags packed and the car loaded with snacks, she and I left just after sunset.

Oh we had such a wonderful road trip listening to sermons, swapping testimonies, talking about our passions, and just enjoying each other's company. She truly is one of the most sacrificial people I know who gives all that she has to her children. Hands down, one of the best moms on the planet!

About half way through the trip, we decided to get a hotel room. It is in my nature to talk with strangers, and with the love of God burning in my heart, I tend to gravitate towards anyone who appears to be downtrodden or hurting. God granted me the gift of encouraging others after that childhood encounter.

Just one word from God can change a person's path in life so it is with great pleasure that I partner with the Holy Spirit to offer prayers and prophetic declarations to encourage others throughout the day. The words we speak over ourselves and others have such power!

Everywhere we went, we felt the love of God flowing through us. The hotel receptionist was no exception that night. So as we checked into the room, feeling blessed to be used by God in so many ways, I drifted off to sleep anticipating the events of the next day when I would come face-to-face with my father.

Divine Paths

The Lord has many ways of confirming when you are walking in His perfect will. Often times, I receive such confirmation through dreams, or through visions that come during the restful state that takes place prior to falling asleep or just before fully waking.

That morning, I awoke from a dream in which my friend was driving very fast around curvy roads. In the dream, I'm holding onto the hand grip of the car because we are sliding around so much, as if on a roller coaster ride. In the dream, we then arrive at my father's house where there are people with wheelchairs and canes who are seeking healing.

My uncle, who often symbolizes Jesus in my dreams, meets to take us to my father. In a whisper, my friend points to my uncle and asks me, "Who is that handsome guy?" I tell her he's known as

"Kingdom Come." We are taken inside and I see my father holding a microphone, about to speak. The dream ends.

Upon waking, I briefly shared the dream with my friend, still meditating on it's meaning. My thoughts were instantly drawn to and stuck on the "Kingdom Come" part of the dream, which reminded me of the Lord's Prayer:

> *"Our Father who art in heaven, hallowed be thy name. Thy <u>kingdom come</u>, thy will be done on earth, as it is in heaven. Give us this day our daily bread. And forgive us our trespasses, as we forgive those who trespass against us. Lead us not into temptation, but deliver us from evil, for thine is the kingdom, the power, and the glory, forever and ever. Amen" Matthew 6:9-13 (emphasis added)*

This gave me further reassurance that the Lord was with me on this trip. As we were turning to cross over a bridge that would lead us into the town my father lived, it was as if a lightening bolt struck my inner core.   Just ahead, my attention was immediately drawn to the name of the bridge, "Kingdom Come."

Wow! Such a profound moment of trust in the Lord swept over me as I knew he was leading my steps. We stopped and prayed, giving thanks to the Lord for his sovereign guidance on the trip. My spine tingled and my stomach fluttered with excitement as we continued, drawing closer to his address.

While entering into the small country town, the GPS revealed that we were about 5 miles away from my father's house. Unexpectedly, I received a call from my sister Jessica. She had stepped outside a store and spotted me just as my friend and I were driving by. How remarkable! *What are the chances of that divine timing?*

Many people may chalk these sort of incidences up to coincidence, but I believe it is the power of God positioning us. The dream actually revealed quite a bit about my father before I ever spent any time with him. I'll expand on that in great detail in the next chapter.

We arranged to meet my sister in the parking lot across from the local gas station and planned to follow her the rest of the way. After hanging up the call, my heart was pumping with excitement because everything was falling perfectly into place!

This was it—reuniting with my father meant so much more to me than I had ever imagined before the trip. It was the culmination of love exuding from my Heavenly Father, who knew just what I needed, matched with the deep-seeded need of that little girl inside of me, desiring acceptance from my earthly father.

After an excited embrace with my sister, and a brief introduction between her and my friend, I was eager to get back on the road. Having Jessica as the lead navigator in the car ahead gave us more assurance of where we were going, especially since the cell phone reception had been spotty in some areas, hindering the GPS navigation.

As we entered into the mountainous terrain, the roads were suddenly filled with winding sharp turns. Jessica had obviously driven these roads countless times and could anticipate the path ahead with confidence, which was reflected in the speed with which she drove.

Following shortly behind her, I found myself needing to grab hold of the hand grip to steady myself around the sharp turns. It was in that moment, the flash of my dream came into full focus!

A flood of love and reassurance rippled throughout my entire body as I realized and felt the manifested presence of Jesus with us. I could sense his sheer delight in the anticipation of me meeting my father. The Lord truly takes pleasure in giving good gifts to his children!

Finally, Jessica's car began slowing down as we followed the turn into the driveway entrance of our father's house. Just ahead, I could see him standing under the porch. I jumped out of the car, and after more than three decades of separation, I found myself melting into the loving arms of my father's embrace.

Any fear I was carrying was instantly swept away, as tears of immense gratitude cascaded down both our faces. My heart was overflowing with pure joy! As I type this now, I envision broken pieces of my heart were joining back into wholeness. Scripture states that Jesus came to bind up the brokenhearted. That's a perfect portrayal of how I felt in that moment.

God's Mercy

I want to take a brief moment to address any hardness of heart that may be causing you to feel anger towards my father as you read this, or someone who may have hurt you or a loved one deeply. Again, I am not excusing the act as acceptable. What he did was absolutely wrong.

What I am suggesting is that in his great mercy, God chose to forgive mankind and provide a way for us to be reconciled back to him, even though we deserved to be thrown into hell for our rebellion against him.

Even after Adam and Eve sinned, God still clothed them. There are certainly consequences for our sinful choices, but in his great mercy, God continues to love us and guide us towards the path of redemption. He never gives up on us!

There's a story in the Bible about a woman who is caught in the act of adultery, which was punishable by stoning the person to death in the Old Testament. When the religious leaders brought the woman to Jesus, they were trying to trap him into going against the law.

In his profound wisdom, Jesus made one simple statement, "He who is without sin among you, let him cast the first stone." One by one, they all began to leave until it was only Jesus and the woman remaining. He then told her, "Now go and sin no more." What amazing mercy and grace our God displays! However, don't mistake his mercy for acceptance. He is a loving Father, which requires him to also be just in his judgements.

Should the adulterous woman have been punished to death for her choice? Let's look at it from another angle. What would cause her to commit adultery, knowing it was punishable by death? The first thought that comes to mind is desperation for attention, which comes from a wounded soul.

My heart also goes out to her for the public humiliation she must have endured. That's certainly pretty severe punishment in my eyes. Again, not excusing her behavior, but something drove her into committing such an act.

I guessed my father must have also been struggling with some painful wounds, disappointments, and guilt for many things that had happened in his life. He had been caught in a cycle of destruction, attempting to fill a void that can only be satisfied by God's unconditional love. When you're in that place, darkness has a way of working through you.

Pet Sins

Demonic spirits thrive on our deep rooted pain. It's their food source. Remember the fruit flies example? The Bible teaches that demons want to make humans their home.

Since they are spiritual beings without bodies, they will use anyone who is in agreement with their lies, to express their personalities. So, unless our whole being is filled with the Holy Spirit, we are susceptible to demonic influence and/or attachments.

Even as Christians, these attachments can take place in our body or our souls (mind, will, emotions) if we have negative thought patterns or repetitive sin in our lives. The Apostle Paul refers to a thorn that was given to him in his side, or a messenger of Satan, that was allowed to torment him, in order to keep him humble.

When I was walking out my faith, after God regenerated my thyroid, I temporarily embraced fear and unbelief a few days after stopping my medication. The moment I entertained the thoughts that I would die without the medication, my body began displaying dangerous symptoms of withdrawal, so I went back on the medication.

When I asked the Lord about it, he said, "The devil is an illusionist and he will make you think you need his solution more than you need My promises." From that moment on, I trusted what the Lord had promised me and no symptoms ever returned.

I also received medical confirmation shortly thereafter, which showed a normally functioning thyroid, even though it had been fully removed by surgery years before. God is able to do mighty things!

As a note of warning, do not read into this story and assume that I'm suggesting you stop or refuse medication without strong confirmation from the Lord. God does provide instant healings, however, he may also release healing as we walk through the process with him.

Remember, he desires relationship with us, but many regard him as a mere vending machine for what they can get from him. We must seek his face before we seek his hand.

I also don't believe God is opposed to doctors. He created them with purpose and they serve a valuable need in the world. The bottom line is we must seek the Lord for guidance before seeking the opinion of doctors.

Otherwise, we are placing doctors above the Lord, which is idolatry. To illustrate the point of demons affect our lives, the Lord gave me a dream. There is much more to this particular dream, however, for the purposes of this book, I'll narrow the view a bit.

In the dream, I am in a busy park filled with people and dogs walking all about and gathered in different groups. Wherever groups of people are gathered, their dogs of varying sizes seemed to resemble one another, as if sharing a common breed line.

There were also many other individuals walking alone and managing multiple dogs at one time. They gave the impression of weariness and appeared to be heavily burdened by all the energy their dogs demanded.

So what can we glean from this portion of the dream?

The pet dogs represent different kinds of sin or demonic spirits. The groups of people gathered together have similarities in sin, be it greed, gossip, unbelief, fear, pride, self-righteousness, or the like, because they are influenced by the same demonic spirit, but to varying degrees. That makes sense because like minded people tend to gather in groups.

Some people are dealing with multiple sins or demonic spirits at once, which completely consumes their energy and causes them to become listless in our lives. This is why Jesus offers the following invitation:

"Come to me, all you who are weary and burdened, and I will give you rest. Take my yoke upon you and learn from me, for I am gentle and humble in heart, and you will find rest for your souls. For my yoke is easy and my burden is light." Matthew 11:28-30 NIV

The Lord also highlighted that the people are taking ownership of the sin, by leashing themselves to the dog(s). This is representative of demonic attachments to our body and/or soul. Remember, it is the mission of demons to make us their home, in order to express themselves. Only through partnership with Holy Spirit can we defeat sin in our lives.

Yes, it is absolutely possible to live free from the slavery of sin! That thought should fill you with hope, not despair. If it makes you feel condemned in any way, then take it as an invitation to go deeper with Jesus because he wants to rid you of that weariness.

Breaking free from the bondage of sin, or demonic influence, is often a gradual process as we learn to walk in the fullness of our identity in Christ. That requires a renewing of our mind through the intake and practice of truths from the Bible, coupled with a personal relationship with Jesus. Both elements are needed for proper guidance.

Personal Reflections

***

Jesus looked at them intently and said, "Humanly speaking, it is impossible. But with God everything is possible."

Matthew 19:26 NLT

Chapter 9: Radical Reconciliation

The next two days at my father's house were truly a gift that I will forever treasure! His stories were drenched with such profound wisdom from above, it truly felt like sitting at the feet of Jesus. My cheek muscles actually burned from smiling so much!

As we listened intently, my friend kept commenting about the similarities between my father and I. It was as if he had raised me my whole life because we were so linked together in our love for and dedication to living for the Lord.

I also learned that my grandparents were devoted servants of God too. Preaching was part of my spiritual inheritance because the same desire to learn and teach others about the Lord burned deep within my spirit, just as it did within theirs.

Like my ancestors, I also had chosen to dedicate my life to go wherever the Spirit of God led me, delivering His messages and doing His will, no matter the personal cost. My father shared so many wonderful stories of how the Spirit of God had moved through our family, bringing healing miracles and revival outbreaks within the community.

If you recall in the Kingdom Come dream, my father was holding a microphone and there were people seeking healing at his house. This is part of the spiritual inheritance that has been passed down to me.

The past three generations of my family have served God as healing ministers—my grandfather, my father, and now me. It likely goes back further, but at the time of this writing, I have not researched it yet. That fascinates me, especially considering I wasn't raised by my father! Often we focus on curses that are passed down through the generations, but blessings are also inherited.

I recently united with my father's sister, who also has an extensive history of healing miracles. It runs in our family because God runs through our family. He is the power source and we are simply his willing vessels.

Our conversations are steeped with stories of how God worked miracles through our prayers. That's what is meant by being an ambassador and co-laborer with Christ!

There is truly nothing that compares to the privilege of releasing God's supernatural power into the world around you! It is an absolute blessing to bless others.

Stepping Stones of Faith

As I was visiting with my father, I shared the story of the first time I stepped out to pray for someone in public. I had only been surrendered to the Lord for about 9-10 months, and I was renting a moving truck.

There was a young guy behind the counter who suffered from debilitating back pain after a recreational accident. He nearly called off work that day because the pain was so bad.

Up to that point, I had witnessed friends and church members healed through prayer, but never a stranger. This was a real test of my faith! He accepted the invitation for prayer so my friend and I put our hands on his back. I offered a short prayer thanking God and then commanded the back to be healed. In that moment, it felt like I had warming gloves on as heat radiated into his back!

The guy was also very surprised by the heat. He gingerly began to test out the movement of his back.

To our pleasant surprise, he had full range of motion, even being able to touch his toes, which he could not do before!

With tears welling up in his eyes, he shouted, "You healed me!" I quickly pointed out that it was *Jesus* who healed him, not me. I was merely the messenger. Jesus alone deserves the praise! That miracle was another stepping stone added to my faith ladder.

Because God is so good, he took things further. Later that evening, my friend and I returned the moving truck and dropped the keys into the overnight slot of the building since the office was closed. About half way back to the house, I realized that I left my personal keys in the moving truck. Oh no!!

We turned around, not knowing what we were going to do, but trusting God would guide us once we got there. When we arrived back at the lot, we found a man waiting by a truck. *Perhaps he could help!*

The man approached us as we got out of the car and asked if we were the ones who ordered a locksmith to unlock a car. *What?* I hadn't ordered anything, but shared how grateful I was to see him!

The locksmith kindly unlocked the moving truck for us so I could retrieve my house keys. Afterwards, we shared the testimony of the Lord healing the guy's back earlier that same morning, and he was energized in asking us for prayer.

So we circled together and prayed for a personal matter in his family and thanked God for all he had done that day. To boot, the locksmith didn't even charge us a dime! God is so wonderful to think of all our needs!

Hurting Church

My father was so tickled to hear how God had been using me, and I could sense it brought a deep measure of peace to his heart knowing I was fully devoted to Jesus.

In my mind though, I began to wonder how my father had fallen so far off track with two godly parents who were steeped in ministry. He was obviously not that same man who had inflicted such deep emotional wounds that fateful summer night. So what caused the derailment?

It was then that our Heavenly Father began to open my eyes to the root cause of perpetual abuse in our society, and the desire for me to spread His message of grace to the perpetrator.

I learned early in my walk that church folks are not immune to sin, evidenced by the history of news accounts on sexual perversion and corruption in the church.

Many of our church bodies today function like a hospital that only manages dis-ease, without allowing the cure—God's power—to flow through it. Instead, they peddle feel good motivational messages designed to keep you coming back. That's an over generalization of course, but you get the point.

God often reveals secrets to babes of the faith, which can be be disregarded by others who have been walking with Christ for much longer. I've learned that it's not the length of time you've walked with Jesus, but how deep you let him in that determines your faith maturity.

In the Spring of 2016, the Lord began showing me dreams and visions about dangerous activities occurring in the church I was attending. Most of the dreams were centered around there being a safety issue where people were being led into dangerous or death situations—often by someone in leadership.

One of the first visions I received was during a gathering of women for a Bible study, many of whom were leaders, or wives of leaders, at the church. This was the same group that had witnessed my experience encountering Jesus on the throne, about five months earlier.

During worship, I saw the outline of an angel in a doorway with a very bright light behind him. The angel is holding someone, and as he begins to walk towards me, I see it is a young girl who is completely limp.

As he draws closer, I focus in on the girl's face and immediately recognize her as a member of the youth group at the church. I had only seen her in passing a couple times, so I couldn't recall her name.

In the vision, the angel stands the young girl up, holding her because she's still limp. I notice she has blood running down her inner left thigh and I can smell the pungent odor of dog poop.

I'm suddenly overcome with feelings of grief for this girl as sexual abuse is highlighted in my spirit. The angel then takes us both up into the air where I can see children of all ages below us. I hear a voice say, "My Church has a lot of hurting children."

God is bring healing and cleansing to the Church first so we can be a source of blessing to the hurting world around us. As Christians, we must address the sinful behaviors and demonic influence in our own lives before it's safe to lead others. It all stems around an intimate relationship with God and his word.

The Weeds

Wounds and lies are planted as weeds in the garden of our souls through traumatic experiences or negative mindsets spoken over us. If these weeds go unaddressed, they begin to grow to the point of choking out the healthy plants in our gardens.

Ultimately, it had boiled down to my father losing his sister to a tragic death at a young age. She was also his best friend so the loss was compounded. Some folks in the town had made comments about how God must have taken the child because of family sin.

That traumatic loss and accusation propelled him into depression and a deep seeded bitterness towards God and others. Without addressing this bitterness and pain, my father began to lash out at others, and as he grew older, that bottled up anger was fueled by dangerous self-medicating and addictive behaviors.

How many of you can relate? I know I can. Before walking with God, many times in my life I have made poor choices in lieu of feeling good in the moment. When life is pressing in on you, for whatever reason, often we just want to escape.

It's no wonder our society is steeped in anxiety and depression, because the temporary escape is made so readily available through the many channels of distractions.

When escaping is not an option, like a wild animal that feels threatened, many will lash out at others to keep them from getting too close. That closeness exposes a person's vulnerabilities, which is scary for someone who isn't ready to deal with the root issue of their pain, or who believes the negative lies that were spoken over them.

After awhile, that fear turns into guilt and shame. Therein begins the cycle of abuse—whether self-inflicted or targeted towards others.

It gave me a new perspective to hear what had caused my father such anguish all those years. I thought back to how I felt about my baby sister when she was born. With an eight year gap between us, she was more like my baby than my sister. I was so enamored by her tiny little features and the way she would laugh when I made silly faces. I helped with feedings and diaper changes, wanting to spend all my time with her.

Growing up, I had a very unique bond with my baby sister, and if anything had happened to her, it would have devastated my young little soul. These thoughts filled my heart with sorrow for my father's pain as he shared the memories of their bond.

Spiritual Maturity

On a side note, I have been on both ends of the stick with giving and receiving harsh remarks relating to God's judgement. Regardless of whether it is true or not, we must always speak through the lens of love. God has a way of putting us in front of the mirror to see the impact of our own words.

Often the best way to learn is through first hand experiences. I know I have and am now grateful for the refining fire that came after those learning experiences. It sure didn't feel good at the time, but sometimes a spiritual spanking from Father God is the discipline we need to keep us on the right path.

Love truly is our greatest weapon and gift in a hurting world. However, love also means bringing correction when needed, of course in partnership with Holy Spirit. We are called to work together as a body of believers because each member has a different perspective with the gifts and talents God has granted them.

Not one person is greater than another in the body of Christ. Some may be more in tuned with identifying God's voice, but we are to spur one another on in our spiritual growth, not seek status or recognition for ourselves. Everything comes from Jesus, so everything must point back to him!

Jesus' death tore the veil which kept common folks separated, and only allowed the religious leaders entry into God's presence. Now, every born again Christian is free to interact with God without the reliance on a priest or pastor.

In no way does this negate the need for church leadership or spiritual mentors. The goal, however, should be to bring believers to maturity in their faith, not just get people saved by accepting Jesus as their

Savior.   He must become Lord over your life to receive the fullness of salvation.

I believe the message of "once saved always saved" is a false teaching designed to keep Christians apathetic in their faith.   Jesus is clear in his message to the Church that he will not accept those of lukewarm faith.   This is further supported by the parable of the ten virgins, where five of them did not keep their lives burning for the Lord, and were therefore refused entry.

That is why the Bible urges you not to harden your heart if you hear God's voice, especially when it comes to repentance.   Draw nearer to him and he will draw nearer to you.   That's a promise!

Looking back over my life, I recognize where God was calling me back to his heart, but I ignored him and continued on embracing sin.   Without proper training, anyone can fall prey to false teachings.   We must test everything by the word of God, even that which comes from your church leaders.

I had believed that just because I knew about Jesus and lived according to what I thought was a "good person," then I would go to heaven.   That is simply not true.   One encounter with the Holy Spirit did not deem me a Christian. A true Christian is someone who *follows* Christ, which means he is the one leading your life.

We cannot "earn" our way into heaven by doing good things. Eternal life is a gift given to those who live their life on earth in surrender to Jesus. Now I believe there are varying levels of surrender, and in conjunction, there are varying levels of heaven. That topic is reserved for another writing assignment though!

Healing Words

On the last day of the visit with my father, I felt a strange heaviness in the air. The sunny skies outside did not match the emotional climate that lingered inside of the house. My father had a look of deep sadness when he invited my friend and I into the upstairs living room. As I sat across from him on the couch, again I could sense such a deep sorrow in his melancholy blue eyes.

However, the moment he began speaking, it was like a healing balm was being slathered over my sunburned soul. I immediately felt the blessing of his words bring a deep peace over my entire being.

With his eyes fixed upon mine, he spoke with such sincerity about the sorrow he felt about what had happened so long ago and for the pain it must have caused me. The open faucet of tears poured down our cheeks as he went on to say how grateful he was that my mother had met Rick, and that God had placed such a good man in our lives to take care of us.

Reflecting back, he indicated that he didn't trust himself to be alone with me after that, so he chose to completely withdraw from my young life. For two years following the traumatic encounter, he professed to being on a mission of self-destruction because of the added guilt and shame that tormented him. He wanted so badly to die.

By the grace of God, he met his new wife and felt a glimmer of hope shine into his life again. Seeing him through God's eyes, she insisted that he had to get right with Jesus before she would consider dating him.

Therein began the restoration process of his wounded soul. God had given him another chance at being a father and blessed him with a family. Today, he is a devoted servant of God filled with gentleness and wisdom. Our bond has flourished rapidly in a relatively short time, and I am privileged to learn from his experiences.

Ironically, even though I felt safer not having to see my father after the incident at nine, there was a strange sense of rejection that stemmed from his complete absence in my life. All the years that followed, I was plagued by thoughts of, *"even your own father doesn't want you,"* which led me to believe I was unlovable.

Now I'm able to recognize those as external thoughts from evil spirits who's primary mission was to destroy my self worth and identity.

In a sweeping motion, it was like my father's heartfelt apology pruned my heart of the rejection and trauma weeds that had resided deep inside for so long. Oh the power in our spoken words!

Thinking back to my days of group counseling for domestic violence victims, I remembered the underlying desire among every survivor and how they so longed to hear the words of a *heartfelt* apology from their abusers.

In that moment, I recognized the rarity of the apology I received from my father, and my heart instantly filled with gratitude towards God, who had orchestrated the whole trip. While I had worked through forgiveness in my own personal time with Jesus, this face-to-face reconciliation brought a much deeper level of healing into my heart.

Renewed Hope

God is able to transform *any* person, no matter how grievous their actions have been. That may offend some who are not ready to forgive, but it is my hope that it will draw the hearts of abusers to know that change is absolutely possible for them.

Anyone who has the desire to change, and is willing to humble himself before Jesus, will be given the opportunity of a new life. God's grace is abundant to those who diligently seek him. He wants no one to perish, but for all to come to repentance so he can then wash them clean with the payment of his precious blood that was shed on the cross.

Jesus came to save the sinners—those who are most in need of help.

Saying you're sorry takes tremendous courage, and when you direct it towards God first, with a repentant heart, it is a true act of worship. Consider the story about a prostitute, who became a disciple of Christ and was the first person to see him after his resurrection. Jesus loves to challenge our human ways of thinking!

In the story depicted in the book of Luke, Jesus is having dinner with a Jewish religious leader named Simon. This woman, known as a prostitute, brazenly walked right into Simon's house. Broken and weeping, she covered Jesus' feet with her own tears and then wiped them clean with her long hair. What a beautiful picture of gratitude!

Jesus read Simon's thoughts, which questioned why he was allowing this sinful woman to even touch him. In his clever way of explaining things, Jesus proceeds to tell Simon a story about two men who were deeply in debt.

One man owed something like $100,000 and the other owed $10,000. When it was obvious that neither of them had the ability to repay the debt, the kind banker—represented by God—forgave them both of the debt they owed.

Jesus asked Simon, "Which of the two debtors would be the most thankful? Which one would love the banker most?" Of course, Simon supposed it would be the one with the greatest debt, and he was right.

Typically those who believe they have only a little to be forgiven of, are the ones who only casually follow Jesus, or operate as cold to lukewarm Christians. However, when you realize God is willing to forgive all that you have done, no matter what it is, your heart will instinctively pour out with extravagant gratitude and worship, exemplifying Christians who are hot or on fire for God.

There's really no point in hiding from God. He sees all that you do anyway and *still* loves you! That doesn't mean he approves of the sin in your life. He simply desires to prune those thorns and weeds so you can walk in the fullness of who he created you to be.

Don't believe that whispering lie that you're not worth saving or that you've done too much to be forgiven! It's a lie straight from hell attempting to keep you from knowing the true power of peace and joy that is available to all who will seek after it with their whole hearts.

Jesus looks beyond cultural standards and goes straight to the heart. He's not impressed with status, appearances, or man's ideas of importance. He searches for a heart that cries out for his love and healing.

Don't let pride or fear hold you back anymore. Father God has his arms opened wide to receive you! If you're feeling a stirring in your heart now to accept the invitation, I encourage you to pray right this moment. Don't wait until it's too late.

O Father God, forgive me for all I've done to hurt you, others, and myself. Forgive my debt of sin and wash my record clean of every evil and fowl thing I've ever done. Jesus, I choose to surrender to you as Lord over my life. Send your Holy Spirit to teach and guide me as a witness for your awesome transforming power. Thank you, thank you, thank you for making me a new creation! Amen.

If you sincerely prayed that prayer, then rest assured that God has sealed you with his Holy Spirit and given you the power to overcome evil in and around your life.

Now begins the journey of renewing your mind to align with the truth of your identity. Your old sinful self will try to lure you back into believing you haven't changed, but don't believe it. You are a new creation. Go live like it!

God renewed and reconciled me and my father after a horrific ordeal. He can and will do the same for you when you diligently seek him. Remember, God's love is the most powerful weapon!

The End of yourself is the beginning of eternal life!

Personal Reflections

Appendix A: Suggested

Prayer Guide

Suggested Prayer Guide

Step 1

Find a quiet place to spend time with the Lord to work through the wounds of your soul. You can spend as little or as much time as you would like, so go at your own pace.

Step 2

Journal what the Lord shares with you. It is often the first thought that comes to mind. This will keep you on task, as well as honor the Lord by recording His words to you.

Step 3

Commit to meet with the Lord on a regular basis, preferably around the same time—like a date! He looks forward to your time together and has much to share with you!

These questions are intended as suggestions to get you started, not as a formula, so be open to Holy Spirit's guidance. God desires a two-way interaction with you!

1. Ask Jesus to draw your attention to an area of your garden that needs pruning or attention (i.e., weeds, debris, rotten fruit)

2. What issue or memory does this relate to in my life?

3. What negative thought am I believing about myself with this issue/memory?

4. When was this negative thought first planted in my soul?

5. Repent for agreeing with the negative thought and ask God to cleanse you of the unrighteous thinking.

6. Who do I need to forgive for believing this negative thought?

7. Choose to forgive and bless the person, then repent for holding bitterness in your heart. Give God permission to remove the root of bitterness from your soul.

8. What truth do you want me to receive about myself in place of the negative thought?

9. Thank Jesus for the seed of truth and ask him to plant it into the garden of your heart.

10. In exchange for all the negative thoughts, ask Jesus what good gift He wants to give you to strengthen your defenses against any attempted return of these negative thoughts?

11. Spend time thanking the Lord!

12. Repeat steps 1-11 as needed.

Personal Reflections

Personal Reflections

Personal Reflections

Personal Reflections

Personal Reflections

Personal Reflections

Personal Reflections

Personal Reflections

ABOUT THE AUTHOR

Angela Attiah is a prophetic minister, teacher, and artist who resides in Illinois. While she carries no formal degrees in theology, she is recognized as being a devoted disciple of Jesus Christ, and one who is deeply committed to living a life led by the Spirit of God.

After multiple life changing encounters with the Lord, Angela founded Kingdom Ally, a ministry of reconciliation that promotes personal growth and spiritual development, with the goal of restoring individuals, families, and communities back to wholeness in God. She does so by engaging both the sacred Scriptures, and the ongoing revelation released through the Holy Spirit.

In addition to writing and teaching, Angela also enjoys creating artistic expressions through photography, painting, fashion, poetry, and songwriting. She adores her three children and dreams of living on a horse ranch.

For more information, please visit www.kindomally.org or www.angelaattiah.com.

847-987-9000 cell

ua@Angela attiah.com

Made in the
USA
Columbia, SC